About the Author

Joanna Philpot lives in Yorkshire, England, with her husband and three children. She has a degree in Children and Playwork from Sheffield Hallam University. She owns and runs Maple + Pea, a baby and children's clothing brand, where, along with her designer, she designs fabrics and turns them into little clothes for little humans. She loves going on adventures with her family and seeking joy in the everyday.

Pregnant in a Pandemic

Joanna Philpot

Pregnant in a Pandemic

Olympia Publishers
London

www.olympiapublishers.com
OLYMPIA PAPERBACK EDITION

A CIP catalogue record for this title is
available from the British Library.

ISBN: 978-1-80074-449-3

This memoir is a truthful recollection of actual events in the
author's life. All opinions are their own and all events, places, and
conversations have been recreated from memory and to the best of
their knowledge.

First Published in 2022

Olympia Publishers
Tallis House
2 Tallis Street
London
EC4Y 0AB

Printed in Great Britain

Dedication

For Andrew, Archie, Rory and Sonny. My absolute dream team. 'I love you more than you will never know.'

Acknowledgements

Thank you to my husband, Andrew, for encouraging me to write this book and forever being my cheerleader in all things creative. Thank you for listening to me read it out countless times and for helping jog my memory when recollecting parts of our story. Your love and support are unfailing and I'm so thankful for you.

Thank you to my magnificent children; Archie, Rory and Sonny. Archie, you would sit on the bed whilst I would type and watch my word count, encouraging me and cheering for me when I reached my next milestone. Thank you for telling me how proud of me you are, it means more than you know. Well done for surviving and thriving through home-schooling. You absolutely smashed it.

Rory, you would sit with me whilst I would type and watch cartoons on the laptop next to me so we could work together. Thank you for your energy, love and humour and for keeping us all going through a crazy year. You handled the pandemic so well. You had a delayed start to preschool because of restrictions, you couldn't see family or friends but you would still start and end each day with a smile.

Sonny, without you there would be no book. Thank you for inspiring me to note down our journey together. I will always remember those cosy nights with you; you in your Moses basket and me on my bed typing away on the laptop.

You're such a smiley and happy baby and we all love you so much. You and your brothers are the best team and your love for each other fills me up.

Thank you to the midwifery team and medical staff at Hull Royal Infirmary and to the East Riding community team, who were involved in my antenatal and postnatal care and for keeping Sonny and myself safe and well. The changes in policy and procedure were forever changing but you kept us informed along the way. You provided online support to all expectant mums when we were unable to always see you in person and for that I'm so thankful, it really helped. You all did a spectacular job of keeping mums and babies safe and I'm so grateful to have been in your care. A special thanks to Michelle, my midwife who got me through labour and Jennifer, the midwife assigned to helping expectant mothers online. Thank you both, you were both exactly what I needed.

A special thanks to my amazing and incredible friends for doing school runs, bringing gifts, sending messages, and being there emotionally when you weren't allowed to be there physically. I hope you all know how much you mean to me and how grateful I am to each and every one of you. I am surrounded by strong and inspiring friends and I cherish you all very much.

A big thank you to my parents, Amber and John, for never letting me think there was anything I couldn't do. Thank you for always supporting, encouraging and loving me. You gave me the confidence to always try.

Thank you to Archie's school and teachers for providing emotional support and delivering online classes throughout an incredibly challenging year. You were always available to us and we're so grateful to how you helped us navigate home-schooling.

Thank you to Olympia Publishers for believing in me and my book and for supporting me in getting it out into the world.

Thank you to my in-laws, Gillian and Brian, for providing a copious number of postal gifts to entertain the children whilst you were unable to see them. It kept them busy whilst I brushed up on year two maths! Thank you to my wider family for always supporting me from afar. Never did I think a global pandemic would delay you meeting my baby but here we are! Thank you for being a support virtually when you weren't able to be physically.

Finally, a huge thank you to anybody who has bought this book! I hope you enjoy reading it, thank you so much for supporting me. I'm so grateful, thank you.

Sonny.

I could never hate 2020, as it bought us you. Doing pregnancy, labour and the newborn days in the current state of the world has been hard. Lone appointments, less appointments, not knowing what Covid meant for pregnant women and our babies. You've hardly met any of your family, no playdates. No showing you off. We've just hidden. It's not a start any of us would have wished for. Except. This year has been full of walks, adventures and togetherness and how beautiful is that? It's been a strange one (and hard at times) but not a horrible one. It's been memorable, special and it brought me my third, darling son.

Introduction

It was the 25th March 2014. I'd just arrived at Hull Women and Children's hospital. I was apprehensive and excited. I had never given birth before, I didn't know what to expect. I was almost two weeks overdue so I came to the hospital for an induction. I was induced and eighty-two hours later, on the 28th March 2014, I had given birth to a son. 9lb 3oz of pure joy.

It was the 25th September 2017. I was watching *Coronation Street* and I felt a few twinges. I sent a text message to my parents who were on standby to take care of my eldest when I went in to labour, and ran myself a shower. I felt calm, in control and handled my contractions at home. Five hours later, I knew the baby was close so we went to Hull Women and Children's.

We arrived at the labour ward and were met by a midwife who showed us to our room. Before we'd exchanged pleasantries, my waters broke, and eight minutes later, on the 26th September 2017, I was holding a brand new, squishy, little human. My second son. All 9lb 3oz of him. Again!

This time it is the 20th October 2020. We are in the midst of a global pandemic. My previous two labours (and pregnancies) had been so different. How this one would compare would be anybody's guess.

This book covers pregnancy and being a parent during the Covid-19 global pandemic of 2020. The differences, the worries and the unknown. Three lockdowns, two stints of home-schooling, lone appointments, highs, lows and everything else in between. It is a personal account of my own experiences. My views, opinions and experiences are my own and not representative of anybody else.

2020, the year the world stood still. Our babies will go down in history.

The language used in this book is indicative of the author who identifies as a woman, therefore pronouns used throughout the text reflect this, without offence intended.

Part One:
Pregnancy

Chapter One
A Positive Pregnancy Test and a National Lockdown

I found out I was pregnant with my third child in February 2020. This was a month before the pandemic had been announced, so I didn't have that initial panic of being pregnant in such uncertain times that I can only imagine a lot of women finding out they were pregnant amidst a global pandemic felt. I had the expected emotions of somebody hoping for a positive test. The excitement, the anxiety, the disbelief (I took about four tests to be sure) and the romanticised images of who this baby would be.

I had bought some home pregnancy tests the day before and I had calculated that the best time to take a test would be that weekend. I figured even if I was pregnant right now, it would be too early to be picked up on a pregnancy test and I should wait at least a few more days. But I couldn't help myself. I had just woken up and I knew that my first morning urine would have the highest level of HCG (human chorionic gonadotropin-the pregnancy hormone) so if I was going to do it today, I'd do it now. Everybody else was asleep, I nipped to the bathroom and took the test. I had the strongest feeling I was pregnant (all three times I've 'known' I was pregnant before I took a test because I had the most vivid dreams. Like, really vivid. Totally and completely bonkers. It's always my first pregnancy sign. With my first pregnancy I didn't know it was a sign, but I remember having them and then the test confirmed it. With the second and third pregnancies, the more bonkers my dreams became the more pregnant I knew I was). As I sat and waited, I began doubting myself and decided I probably wasn't pregnant after all and it was my mind playing tricks on me. Then I thought even if I was pregnant, which I probably wasn't, it would be too early to tell and I wondered if I had gone and wasted a test. I did a lot of thinking and had a lot of doubt whilst waiting for the stick to be ready!

Less than three minutes went by and I took a sneak peak at the test. I'm very impatient, can you tell? There was the absolute faintest line I have ever seen. I had to squint so hard to make it out, but it was there. There was a line. I was pregnant. I couldn't believe it! I came out of the bathroom and woke up my husband, Andrew, to tell him. I shoved the wee soaked stick at him (so gross) and bounced up and down. He said he couldn't see anything. He turned the main light on, squinted, held it up to the window and still maintained he couldn't see a thing. He said if I was that sure then he believed me. I knew he didn't think I should get my hopes up, but I knew it was a line. I knew it.

That morning I did the school run covertly giddy and completely oblivious to how different this pregnancy would be. If only I'd known what was about to unfold. Any ideas of how the pregnancy and newborn days were going to look would have been swiftly quashed.

The following day I took another test and the faint line became ever so slightly darker. After this test, Andrew agreed he could see something too. The day after that I took another and the day after another. I decided I may as well use up the tests I'd bought. Each test became progressively darker and we both knew I was definitely pregnant. We went on Google to work out our estimated due date (mid-October 2020) and we began getting excited and started really looking forward to autumn and the new life it would bring.

The morning sickness kicked in fairly swiftly. This was my third rodeo, I knew what to expect, but it doesn't make it any more tolerable does it? My morning sickness was actually different with all three babies. With my first, I had it for about eighteen weeks. I would wake each morning, be sick and then I instantly felt better and I could get on with my day. So it lasted quite a while, and being sick is never nice, but it made it a lot easier to deal with as I actually felt fine after I'd vomited and didn't have very much nausea at all. With my second baby, it lasted twelve or thirteen weeks but I was never sick. Just nauseous. I found this so much worse than my first as it meant I would spend all day just feeling sick. Everything made it worse; food, smells, movement. It was grim.

With this baby, I had a mixture of the two. My morning sickness lasted about twelve weeks and I had a combination of all day nausea interspersed with the odd period of throwing up. Isn't pregnancy glamourous? Those first few weeks are rough!

Soon after we found out I was pregnant, we went to visit my parents to share our good news. My eldest son, Archie, had drawn a picture of himself with my other son, Rory, and a baby. He had actually drawn three of these pictures. One each to announce the pregnancy to both sets of grandparents and one for us to keep, which is now framed and displayed on our bedroom wall.

I remember later on that day, when we were at my parent's house and we'd shared our good news, my mum and I watched a news report on Covid-19 and we had a discussion about if the other was worried about it spreading to this side of the world. We both naively dismissed it. We were deeply saddened over the devastation it was causing in China, but we had no inkling that it would soon become our reality too. You couldn't escape news of Covid-19 (also referred to as Covid and Coronavirus), whether it was on the news or social media, but it still didn't seem like it would affect us directly.

After watching the news and discussing all things Covid, we went back to talking about baby names, baby clothes and my due date. We spoke about baby showers, christenings and all things baby. It was such early days but we were incredibly excited and couldn't help ourselves. We video called Andrew's parents later that day too, to share our news and at that point we were still very much, naively and comfortably, in our pregnancy bubble. We had no idea how the next few weeks would unfold and what our future would look like.

Covid-19 is an infectious disease that was first reported to the World Health Organisation at the end of 2019.

Most people who contract the virus will experience mild to moderate respiratory illness but for some, it is fatal.

The virus spreads through saliva or by coughing or sneezing. The main three symptoms, which if experienced require immediate testing, are a new and continuous cough, a fever and a loss or change of your sense of smell. Other symptoms include aches, pains, sickness, diarrhoea, headaches, a rash, difficulty breathing and chest pain.

The epicentre of the outbreak of Covid-19 was in Wuhan, China. We had heard all about it on the news, but nobody could have predicted the next twelve months and beyond. They were just so unprecedented. It was like a movie and a nightmare come true. We would hear and see reports on Covid daily but I don't think anybody appreciated how serious it was or how serious it would become. We had just heard about a 'new virus' in China. We knew it was serious, but we didn't really know much else. It moved fast though and it wouldn't be long before we knew much more and it would have a deep impact on all of our lives.

On the 23rd January 2020, The Foreign and Commonwealth Office advised against essential travel to Wuhan. It was at this point that the seriousness of the situation was unravelling. Still, it seemed so far away, geographically and figuratively. At this point, most of us were still on the outside looking in. A few days later, British citizens living in Wuhan were offered flights back to the UK. On the 28th January 2020, the Foreign and Commonwealth Office advised against all essential travel to China. The following day, British Airways suspended all flights going in and out of mainland China with immediate effect. It was getting very serious very quickly. On the 29th January 2020 the first two British cases of Covid-19 were confirmed. Not only had Covid come to the United Kingdom, but the patients were being treated at the hospital my husband worked in, in the village we lived in. There was no denying it was becoming our reality now. The next month showed cases and fatalities rising at an exponential rate.

On the 11th March 2020, the World Health Organisation declared the outbreak of Covid-19 a global pandemic.

Nothing immediately changed for us, just musings on what the next steps would be and what this meant for everybody. I spent the next few days concerned, worried and on tenterhooks; waiting for our next instructions. On the 16th

March 2020, the government advised against all unnecessary contact. Vulnerable groups, including pregnant women, were included in those that should take extra care and be extra vigilant. I phoned school the following day and told them I was taking Archie out of school. I was sure people might think I was overreacting, but I wasn't going to send my son to school when we'd been told to avoid contact with people. Not until we knew more anyway. Nobody had any idea how the virus would affect pregnant women and our unborn children, never mind our 'earth-side' children, so I just wanted to hide away and keep us all safe. I phoned school and told them I would teach my son from home until we knew more about what was happening. I explained that I was newly pregnant and I didn't know what the virus meant for the baby and that I couldn't take any risks. The school staff agreed and were happy that until we heard more from the government, to keep him off with no repercussions. It turns out teaching from home is exactly what we would all be instructed to do for the foreseeable anyway.

The day after, on 18th March 2020, our prime minister, Boris Johnson, instructed schools around the country to close (to all children except those of keyworker parents; that is parents who must continue to work such as healthcare workers and essential shop workers) and a few days later on the 23rd March 2020, the government chose to 'lockdown' the entire country. This meant, aside from shopping for essentials, medical emergencies, one walk a day, and going to work if you couldn't work from home, people were not able to leave the house. Children had to learn from home via remote teaching, many workers were furloughed and people were panicked (remember when there was no flour or loo roll on the shelves?). Everything closed. Non-essential shops, cinemas, places of worship, schools (to non-keyworker children), hairdressers, beauty salons, sport venues, gyms, studios, art galleries. Everything besides the essential. It was very real now.

The one thought that was persistently whirling around my head was the uncertainty of if and how pregnant women and their unborn children were affected. It goes without saying what a worry it was keeping my children and husband safe, but my baby hadn't formed or developed yet and this virus was so new, nobody knew if and how they would be affected if a pregnant woman was to contract it. Would it cause a miscarriage, early labour, birth defects or would the baby be completely safe tucked up in their cosy cocoon? Nobody knew and my anxiety was sky high.

Because of this, we gave Andrew the job of designated food shopper (it made sense as he had to go out to work anyway, so he would go whilst already out) and I would hibernate at home with the children. The times I would go out, for our allotted one-hour exercise we were permitted, I would truly panic each time another person walked past me. In a strange attempt of keeping me and my unborn child safer, I would turn my head and hold my breath. I knew it would be ineffective and pointless to do this, but so many people I have spoken to say they did the same thing. Anything to keep the germs at bay. I was paranoid of everybody. I could see the virus everywhere. I was scared of my own shadow and the whole situation was beginning to take a real toll on my mental health. I was also fully making a conscious effort not to let my children see this. I needed to protect them too, physically and emotionally. Archie had taken it all in his stride but one day he was at school with his classmates, the next we were telling him he wasn't allowed to go to school and we all had to hide out at home. He kept asking how long for but we couldn't give him an answer. It was a lot. I feel incredibly lucky though to have had my husband here to take on all that I couldn't. Our situation afforded us to be able to have Andrew go to the shops and anywhere essential, whilst I stayed home with the children, and I will always be grateful for that and it isn't lost on me what a fortunate position I was in.

When the country was in this lockdown (that's right, this would not be the first time), was when I first started feeling the effects of being pregnant in a pandemic. The routine midwife appointments now had to be taken over the phone, nobody had a clue if we (the pregnant women) were more at risk or not and panic started to set in. My entire pregnancy was about to be completely different to my others, I just didn't know how.

Just weeks prior to the outbreak, I had been Googling pregnancy yoga and antenatal swimming classes. I had suffered from SPD (symphysis pubis dysfunction) and sciatica in my previous pregnancies and I wanted to keep as healthy and mobile as possible before it potentially set in again. I was determined that as soon as I had reached twelve weeks, I would start some classes. Unsurprisingly, these classes never happened and that was just the beginning of what pregnancy in a pandemic would look like.

I heard a saying during this time which stuck with me and fast became my mantra. 'Same storm, different boat'. Everybody in the entire world would be affected by the current climate, but for me, it was how to deal with being a mother to two small people and pregnant to another. It would be about how I would navigate home-schooling, whilst dealing with sickness and generally being pregnant and being a playmate to a toddler too, who had no idea what was going on besides getting to have his best friend off school each day. Rory was ecstatic!

Days went by and although never officially on the 'shielding' list (a list devised by the government of the most vulnerable people likely to become severely unwell if they caught Covid, who were advised not to leave the house at all during lockdown), I chose to spend my days inside as much as possible. I was fortunate that I work from home and the schools had closed, so I didn't *have* to go anywhere. I work designing and making baby clothes (Maple + Pea). It has always been a job that I have been able to work around my children so this wouldn't change. I felt incredibly grateful for that. It was a brand and a job I created after having my first son and I would generally work on evenings and at weekends. I would still be able to work this way, perhaps just slower to accommodate home-schooling and an ever-expanding stomach; but I could work as normal and take maternity leave when I was ready. I took this time to add some new makes for my unborn baby and other two, to make in between orders. My baby would be kitted out, head to toe, in clothes I had designed and made for them and that was an incredible feeling! And obviously I made a bunch of matching clothes for all three of them to wear, I couldn't help myself.

Google searches were coming up blank when I would hopelessly try and find the answer as to whether my baby was at risk and what I could do to protect them, so I chose the safest option and stayed indoors as much as possible. I had never wanted a window to the womb as much as I did now. I needed to see if the baby was safe. I needed to know. That, and to hibernate under my duvet cover for the next seven months. But even then, I was terrified of the baby coming in to the world and being exposed to the virus and put at even more risk. It was all so new, nobody had answers and it was all really very worrying.

Chapter Two
The First Antenatal Appointment

AFTER I had taken my pregnancy tests and confirmed I was pregnant, I phoned the GP to let them know and they gave me the number for the midwives. I presume each trust does it differently, but here you self-refer. It's amazing what you forget in between pregnancies, so I just phoned the GP first to see what I had to do. I phoned the midwives, they took my details and estimated approximately how far along I was and then booked me an appointment to see them when I would be around nine weeks pregnant.

Andrew was off work that day, so he had the children whilst I went to my appointment. The appointment was a very standard admin type affair and no different to any other booking appointments I'd had. The midwife was in full PPE (personal protective equipment) as a precaution and I remember asking her how worried I should be about Covid and how it would affect the pregnancy. She was very calm and seemingly confident that it was all precaution and that there was no need to worry too much. Although we were in the midst and very beginning of a pandemic, she and I both felt quite calm at this point and had absolutely no idea of the impact it would have on everyone. It was new, we thought it would go away as quickly as it had come and we were both incredibly naive and optimistic. There was no conversation about how labour would be amongst a pandemic, how life with a newborn in a pandemic would be, about who could and couldn't visit, because quite frankly, we didn't expect it to go on for that long and we thought and hoped we would just have to ride it out for a little while.

The midwife weighed me, measured me, took blood and urine and wrote all the information down she needed from me. She gave me a pregnancy folder and my pregnancy notes and whilst I was sat there, she phoned the sonography department at the hospital to book an appointment for my twelve-week scan. The week I was estimated to be twelve weeks pregnant (which is when your first standard NHS scan is, also known as a dating scan) also happened to be the week of my wedding anniversary. She asked if any day was better than any others and I asked her if it was possible could she make it on the date of my anniversary. She could, she got us booked in and I was so excited to tell my husband that we would be going for a scan on our anniversary. In hindsight, this was probably not the best idea; had we received bad news I'm not sure I would have wanted to associate our wedding anniversary with that, but at the time we were completely happy and giddy that we could look forward to the very best way to celebrate. Last year's takeaway and movie night would have nothing on seeing our baby for the first time!

Chapter Three
The Twelve Week Scan — Alone

ON 14th April 2020, I went to the hospital for my twelve-week scan. I say 'I', because pregnant women had no choice but to go alone. That day was our wedding anniversary. I remember waking up and instead of feeling joyous, excited and terrified; I just felt terrified.

The weeks preceding the appointment, Andrew and I were looking forward to being able to celebrate our anniversary by going to the scan together. We had been counting down the days and it was just an incredibly exciting, albeit nerve-racking, time. Just a week or so before the scan, we received a letter stating nobody would be allowed to come in with me. Only the pregnant person could attend (unless with a carer) and there would be no exceptions. It was all to keep the women and staff safe, I fully appreciate that, but it was heart breaking and terrifying. Women shouldn't have to be alone for their scans.

We decided that Andrew and the children would all take me to the hospital and would wait for me in the car. My children had to come with us as unless you had a 'childcare bubble' which was a dedicated family or person able to be your childcare, you didn't have any choice. We couldn't drop them off at a neighbour's house as they all had their own childcare bubbles with their children and grandchildren, and you weren't allowed to double up. I have no doubt we could have found a friend without an existing bubble that would have helped us out without faltering, but as Andrew couldn't come in anyway and we were still so nervous about unnecessary contact, we decided to just to bring them with us. If it was bad news, I wouldn't have wanted to drive home alone, so Andrew driving me to the hospital made sense.

We decided I would text Andrew from inside the hospital if it was good or bad news. If it was bad news, he needed to know before I got back in the car as it would be a conversation we couldn't have in front of the children. Imagine that. Imagine if it was bad news and that's how my husband had to find out. Imagine being that woman having absolutely zero support with her and needing to text the most devastating news to her person. Imagine being that partner sat in a car with his other children staring at his phone waiting to see if it was good or bad news. I felt that maternity had been completely forgotten about. Particularly later on when other capacities were opening back up and allowing people to mix.

I walked in to the hospital, notes in hand, face mask on (at this point, face masks weren't mandatory but I wanted to wear one) and before I was allowed in, I had to have my temperature taken and sanitise my hands. My temperature was fine so I could enter the hospital. I found where I needed to go and checked myself in. It was amazing how face masks soon became the norm. When I wore one for my scan, I felt slightly self- conscious. Except for the staff, there was only one other woman wearing a mask. Fast forward just a few more weeks and they became mandatory and it was considered unusual to see people without them.

There was tape on the floor to make sure people could

32

'social distance' (keep two meters apart), every other chair had been turned around so you weren't able to sit too close to anybody and the staff were in full PPE. I sat down on a chair and could not stop my leg from shaking. I thought I was going to pass out. Not only was I terrified of hearing bad news, but this was the first time I had left the house (walking outside for exercise with the children aside) in weeks. My husband was doing the shopping, there was no school, so apart from to get fresh air, we weren't allowed out anyway.

I was desperate for a wee (you are told to up your fluids in order for the sonographer to get a clear image of the baby), I was in a white, clinical waiting room, with tape and signs everywhere, staff in masks and it just wasn't a relaxing or calm environment at all. Getting used to people in facemasks was hard; it's amazing how much I found myself needing to see people's mouths to hear what they were saying. It was a really anxious time. I can't imagine how difficult it must have been for those hearing impaired and not being able to lip read.

My name was finally called out, and I followed the sonographer to the room I would have a glimpse of my baby for the first time in. I handed her my notes, and laid down in the dimly lit room. The sonographer explained that she would put some gel on my tummy (it was never cold like I always expected) and she got her wand and moved it across my stomach. Almost instantly she turned the screen so I could see, and I saw my little baby's heart beating. This wasn't the first time I had seen one of my children dancing around on a monitor but it would never not be magical. It would be the first time I wouldn't have my husband's hand to hold whilst staring at awe at the screen, but it was still incredibly special and just the most magical experience.

The sonographer took some measurements, gave me an estimated due date of 15th October 2020, and did some checks. She printed off some photographs of our little Pumpkin (this affectionately became our nickname for the baby), gave me some paper towel so I could wipe down my stomach, and I hopped off the bed.

It was good news. Baby was healthy. I sent my husband a brief text to tell him this whilst working out where to go next (I had to have routine bloodwork done). Whilst I was sat in the waiting room though, I saw a woman through the double doors, in tears. It didn't take a rocket scientist to work out why she was so distraught. She was alone. Nobody could comfort her, could hold her. It was inhumane. I am *so* sorry if you were one of these women. A woman finding out your baby was poorly or had died and had to be alone whilst finding this out.

Having to go to a follow up appointment to decide the next steps, alone. It was abhorrent that this had to happen and I am so sorry it did.

Chapter Four
An Online Community

AFTER I'd had my twelve-week scan, I went on Facebook and typed 'Due in October' in the search bar. I joined one of the groups that popped up and I am so glad I did. The group consisted of hundreds of women, pregnant, in a pandemic, and due at the same time as me. These women were going through the exact same as me and it was so nice to be able to have an online community of women I could relate to. I didn't post terribly often, but I would contribute and make friends and would later find out that a handful of them lived locally. It became a safe space for us to rant, vent, cry, laugh and share with women who truly understood what each other was going through.

The group was a real mixed bag of mums. Some first time, some seasoned. Some working, some not. Some with their partners, some not. Some young, some not as young. We made friends, swapped stories and if we had a question, it was a great place to ask as chances were somebody knew the answer or had just been through the same thing.

Whilst we were all still pregnant, we were all anxious and apprehensive of what labour would be like in the current climate. We were under different hospital trusts so it wouldn't be exactly the same for everybody, but it was so comforting having people in the same situation.

Now all the babies are here, the group is mainly used to share cute anecdotes or adorable photos, but it is also used to share our anxieties over Covid. We will write about being sad that our babies can't meet anybody, that they can't go swimming or that they can't go to a baby class. We will support each other when the postnatal hormones mixed with 'Covid anxiety' is just too much and we need somebody who can fully relate. The mums on there with school aged children will use the platform to vent if home-schooling whilst being a 24/7 milk bar to a newborn is too much that day. It's a fantastic support network and I'm so thankful for social media and technology to get us through this unnerving time. A lot of us don't get to see another adult very often if at all at the moment, so having these pocket friends has become a life line and a crutch I, and so many, heavily rely on.

Chapter Five
My Sixteen Week Midwife Appointment, Over the Phone

APART from my 'booking' appointment that I had had at around nine weeks, this was my first real midwife appointment. The booking in appointment was just admin, this would be the first appointment, post scan.

Like all appointments at the moment, unless the health care professional needed to see you, it would be done over the phone or via video call. The midwife phoned me for what I thought would be a routine conversation. It was my third pregnancy, I hadn't had any prior complications and there was nothing I was concerned about this time either. Aside from the obvious.

Prior to this appointment, Andrew and I had discussed where I would like to give birth. It was still early days and nothing needed to be decided just yet, but we thought it wise to discuss our plan with the midwife so she knew where we were at too. My two previous births were both in hospital and both relatively straight forward (we'll forget the 'not quite week long but felt like it' induction I had with my first). Because of this and because of the current global situation, Andrew and I decided a homebirth might be a favourable option. It would limit the amount of people (germs) around me and my newborn, we didn't need to worry about childcare for my other two children and overall, it seemed like the safest and right option for us. We began researching homebirths, were happy with everything we read and heard and we decided that is what we would do.

The midwife phoned for my sixteen-week appointment (whilst I simultaneously and desperately tried distracting my two-year-old with the iPad/snacks/toys/any bribe I could conjure up; why is it when you're on the phone the toddler must immediately try and speak to the other person, hang up, or be as loud as they can?!). I was told that when I handed in a urine sample seven weeks ago, it had shown that I had GBS (Group B Strep). Initially, a few weeks previous to this, the doctor had phoned me and said I had a urine infection and I was prescribed antibiotics. I thought it was a standard urine infection and didn't think anything else of it, but the midwife said it was GBS and was surprised I hadn't been told. I don't blame anybody personally for the miscommunication or misunderstanding, but this shows what pressure the NHS was already under and lockdown had only just begun.

The midwife didn't actually tell me I had GBS, she said "…oh and as you have GBS…" I had to stop her and say I had no idea that I did, I hadn't been told this and what the heck does this mean for me and my baby?! She was lovely, apologetic and it wasn't her fault. She gave me some initial facts and I went off to Google later that day to do my own research.

I am allergic to penicillin, and that is the antibiotic of choice to treat GBS (whilst in labour) so I began researching alternatives. As usual with me when leaving an appointment, I thought of all the questions surrounding this after the midwife had hung up. I was very thankful to the wealth of information available to me online to research how the baby and I would be treated instead.

So you know that ideal and safe homebirth plan I had? Because I had GBS, it was now advised I give birth in hospital so I could have a drip of antibiotics whilst doing so, to protect the baby. The idea is that as soon as you have a contraction you go in to hospital to be put on the drip, so you can receive enough of the medication before the baby comes which will in turn protect the baby.

Given that this was my third baby (and they usually come quicker than the last) I knew I had a very small window of getting to the hospital in time so I'd have to be ready to go as soon as labour began. My whole 'I'll give birth at home so I don't need to worry about childcare' plan went out the window and now I had to work out who could have them, as soon as labour began, so we could go to the hospital. Ah well. I knew we would find a solution for the bigger two but I was honestly petrified of having a newborn in a germy hospital. Of course there are always choices, but in this particular scenario, I didn't feel like I had a choice and I knew the safest place for baby (in terms of GBS) was in the hospital. What a choice, eh? I was thankful that the infection had been caught early as I now knew my baby had less chance of becoming ill. A lot of women don't know they have GBS and if passed on to the baby, it can be serious and life threatening.

I had asked the midwife about the glucose tolerance test that I presumed I would have to have, as I did with my other two pregnancies. With my other pregnancies, because of family history, I had to be tested (by a glucose tolerance test) for gestational diabetes. The test involved going in to hospital, having some blood taken, drinking a disgusting glucose drink and waiting a few hours for it to go around your system before having more blood taken. They were the most laborious appointments but ones which were necessary in order to keep the unborn baby (if the test came back positive) and yourself healthy and well. The tests both came back negative with my first two pregnancies but it didn't mean it would for a third time and I still presented with a risk factor so I presumed I would have to be tested again.

When I asked the midwife about the test and if I needed to be booked in for one, she said because of Covid, they weren't doing them. This was a huge (and worrying) surprise, but they didn't want pregnant women waiting around in the hospital unnecessarily and were cutting all none essential appointments and contact. Instead, they would take your blood when you would next be seen in person and you would be tested that way. I'm not entirely sure how it worked and how and why they did it the other way if this way worked too, I just know that's the way they did it this time. I was lucky, for the third time I didn't have gestational diabetes.

Chapter Six
Baby Visiting Logistics

PRE-COVID, when you had a baby, it was very normal to expect an influx of visitors. Whether it be short and sweet visits to have a cup of tea, meet the baby and wish you well, or whether it's longer, out of town family coming to meet their new relative. Of course everybody is different, some people love visitors and want as many as possible celebrating your new little life and some want to hibernate for a little while longer and leave seeing people until a little later on. Whatever your preference, before the pandemic, it didn't seem so much of a worry and there was no real need for too much planning and it certainly wasn't anything to excessively worry about.

When the pandemic began, and the realisation that you were about to bring a brand new, tiny human in to a world where the whole globe was isolating and hiding from a deadly virus, well the thought of people visiting your brand-new baby was utterly terrifying. The laws and restrictions kept changing so it was impossible to even know if anybody would be allowed to visit, never mind if you wanted anybody to. We couldn't really plan, just postulate, but it was a conversation frequently had and we wanted to make the best decision for everyone.

All over my due date group were women asking the same question. 'Are you letting family members meet your baby and if so, when?' We were all panicked and all at a loss. We had been told to isolate, to keep safe and everything we were doing was to keep the baby as safe as possible. It had been ingrained. It just didn't compute that once the baby was born and exposed to the elements that we could then share them with the world.

My friend, who was pregnant and at a similar gestation to myself, and I would have this conversation an awful lot. The month she was due she still didn't have an answer. Neither did I. I wanted my family to meet my baby so much, but I was scared. I didn't want to put my baby or my other children at risk and neither option was sitting right with me. Saying no visitors made me feel guilty, allowing visitors made me feel scared. It was a really horrible situation and my husband and I spoke about it, at length, for ages. I am a big believer in listening to my gut but our guts weren't giving us the answer this time and we had no idea what to do for the best.

I had a lengthy conversation with my health visitor about what the rules were in regards to having visitors once the baby was here. She reminded me that currently it wasn't allowed as people weren't allowed in your house anyway and that a garden or window meeting may be possible, but nothing else was allowed. She pointed out that if these rules were still in place when the baby was born, that I didn't need to worry about making any decision as the law will have done that for us anyway. We had asked my mum if she would be able to be here to take care of my other children when I was to go in to labour, so she (and my dad when he picked her up) would meet the baby as a product of that, but aside from that we didn't know how it would play out. We decided to stop planning, stop worrying and to see what the guidance was at the time of the baby being born. We'd let the law decide and go with that, and our gut, when the time came. As it happened, strict restrictions were in place so nobody was allowed to meet the baby anyway. I needn't have worried so much as the decision had been taken out of our hands. It still sucked though. We didn't get to share our new joy with anybody and that was really rough.

Although we felt slight relief that the decision had been made for us, it felt incredibly sad that our baby wouldn't get to meet any of their family for a really long time. We didn't expect the baby to have to go without meeting family for quite as long as they did. We had assumed that even if we couldn't have people over, we could have door step visits or a walk in the park. We would have had no way of knowing that even that wouldn't be allowed for people living out of the area. When the baby was born, the current guidance was that unless for work or in a support bubble, you were not allowed out of your village or town. The message was clear, to stay at home or at least very close to home as much as possible.

We had no idea how long it would be before our baby would meet anybody and that was incredibly sad.

Chapter Seven
A Private Scan, an NHS Scan and a Gender Reveal

A few weeks prior to my twenty-week scan, I went for a private one. It's something we hadn't done in my previous pregnancies, but we decided we'd find out the sex of the baby early this time and have a fun little reveal. It was for Archie and Rory really, there wasn't a lot to do these days so we thought it would be fun and give us all something to look forward to. Andrew was technically allowed to come to this scan as amazingly, the private clinics were allowing one other person in with you. However, because there was no one we had formed a childcare bubble with, there was nobody to watch the children, so again, the three of them waited in the car. Most or even all of our friends and neighbours had already formed childcare and support bubbles and our families lived too far away, so it was hard to find anybody to help. Even if we could have found somebody to help, we were reluctant to ask as we were still incredibly nervous about, well, people! It was to keep others safe as well as ourselves; my husband works in a busy hospital and we were nervous about passing germs to people and vice versa. We honestly just wanted to bubble wrap ourselves.

I went in to the clinic (Hey Baby Hull) which was Covid secure and it was an incredibly relaxed environment. It was a 'one in, one out' system so me getting there early was to my disadvantage as I had to wait outside until I was invited in. I queued outside and waited. When it was time for my appointment, the door was unlocked, I was warmly greeted and I was asked to sit down in the first room. The room had two doors and was being used as a sort of air lock, so whilst the other woman was finishing up, I was being kept completely separate. I was handed some forms and was asked to fill them out. There were questions about any potential Covid symptoms I was exhibiting (I wasn't) and if I was to not be at the appointment. There were also questions about my pregnancy and they asked if I would like to find out the sex of the baby. I ticked yes! I was too impatient and too excited. I think women who don't find out are amazing! I could never wait!

I had my facemask on, had sanitised my hands and patiently waited to be called in for my scan. I was called in to such a lovely and inviting room. There was the bed that I would lie on, a settee which would be for family members to watch (had they been allowed) and a huge screen to view the baby. There was a light which turned the room pink or blue after confirming the sex and the sonographer was completely lovely. I was really excited. I didn't have any anxiety (apart from the usual hoping my baby was okay) and I was just so happy to be there. I lay on the bed, just as I did for my dating scan, and was asked to lift up my top whilst the sonographer put some gel on my tummy. She moved her wand over my stomach, and we instantly saw my little baby kicking, stretching and yawning.

Hilariously (and probably frustratingly for the sonographer) the baby kept wriggling, and it was so hard for the sonographer to see if they were looking at a baby boy or a baby girl. They decided it was most likely a boy, and told me if I found out at the NHS twenty-week scan that they were wrong, to let them know, but they were almost certain with their findings. We had paid for a couple of extras including some video footage and a sound recording of the baby's heartbeat, so I laid there whilst the sonographer collected all of that. We got some amazing video footage of the baby wriggling around and the sonographer promised me that it would be emailed to me later that day. I was so excited to show my husband and children! We got a great recording of the heartbeat, which would then be put in to a soft toy so that when we squeezed it, we could hear the baby's heart beating.

I wiped the gel off of my stomach, picked up my bag and maternity notes (I didn't know if I would need them or not, I didn't) and went in to the third room where there was a receptionist waiting and a room full of soft toys and gender reveal paraphernalia. I had already paid for a gender reveal canon, so I picked one up that said 'it's a boy' which would be full of blue smoke and confetti and I chose my stuffed toy for the heartbeat to be placed in to. I chose a cute, little lion and handed it to the receptionist for her to put the sound recording in to.

Although Andrew wasn't able to be at the scan, it was amazing to be able to show him the video footage of baby wriggling around and to be able to hear their heartbeat too. Although we were almost/probably/pretty much definitely sure that baby was a boy, we wanted to wait until our twenty-week scan to check. We decided to keep the canon to one side and patiently waited until our next NHS scan to confirm. Although Andrew and I knew baby was probably a boy, at the next scan it would only be me (and the sonographer) who would know for sure so I would do the gender reveal after that. More of a gender double check than a gender reveal, but it was incredibly fun none the less.

Apart from wanting to do a fun gender reveal for our children, we also opted for a private scan because our hospital (in fact most hospitals around the UK) were not allowing you to video your NHS scan on your phone.

There were petitions and campaigns fighting against this, as all pregnant women wanted was to be able to share their scans, even if only remotely. Partners (or anybody — friends or family) were unable to see their unborn child at a scan, so the least we (pregnant women nationwide) had hoped for was to be able to get a little clip of the baby wriggling around. It didn't seem too much to ask. The reason we were given for this to not be an option was because the mother needed to lay still for the sonographer to get an accurate scan. Our argument was that we could wait for all the essential measurements and checks to be done until we got a ten second video clip of the baby. They still would not budge. It wasn't fair and I know a lot of pregnant women and their partners struggled with this. We appreciated the (now free) photographs we would get and be able to share, but our partners wouldn't be able to see their baby wriggle around on screen so it was a shame we weren't allowed to film our scan for just a few seconds.

A few weeks later, I went to our NHS twenty-week scan. At this point, face masks were mandatory and the hospital had upgraded their temperature checking system from an ear thermometer to an automatic scanner which I didn't realise I was walking through. I walked through the doors, was told to hand sanitise and I asked if they needed to take my temperature. They pointed to a sensor and said they already had!

We had the same system as before. My husband and children would wait in the car, and I would text to say if it was good or bad news. This scan was the anomaly scan, so the sonographer would be checking that the baby was developing properly, where the placenta was lying (mine was attached to the front of the uterus-anterior) and for any rare conditions that the baby may have. It is a long and thorough exam and again, it felt so sad that I had to be alone. Of course, rules like this were being put in place to protect mothers, babies and everybody else. It was still hard though, when women were still made to go to maternity appointments alone. You had to go in to the hospital alone, wait in the waiting room alone and have your scan alone. It just felt incredibly unfair. The mothers, and their baby's health and safety were at the forefront of everybody's minds and I absolutely and completely appreciate why the hospitals were in no rush to allow partners back in to the hospitals, but when you were living it and scared and anxious, it was still incredibly difficult.

I had a very lovely and sympathetic sonographer which was particularly poignant as I needed that. I would have preferred my husband holding my hand but I think the kind health care professionals will always stand out at a time like this. Everybody was living a nightmare and we were all scared. Kind individuals made the world of difference and were always remembered.

As before, I handed the sonographer my maternity notes and hopped on the bed. I lifted up my top and had the warm gel squirted on my stomach. The wand glided over my tummy, the sonographer checked for the heartbeat and she turned the screen towards me so I could see the little one wriggling and dancing around. She very quickly confirmed that baby was a boy. I was so happy and couldn't wait to let the others know. I was most definitely a boy-mum now and I couldn't have been happier. I'd have been ecstatic either way, but I spent the rest of the scan daydreaming about my third son, what he would look like, what we would name him and my team of little guys. I was so, incredibly happy.

I was told I had an anterior placenta (my other two pregnancies I had posterior placentas) and was assured it was nothing to worry about as it wasn't laying too low (which would have been cause for concern), but I might not feel movements as strongly or for a while. She said often ladies with anterior placentas end up in hospital more frequently to have their baby's movements checked because they are harder to feel, which causes worry and concern, but if that was the case then not to put it down to me having an anterior placenta and to come straight in. As it happened, I felt the baby kick as normal and there were no periods of lack of movement. I would never have known my placenta was in a different position had I not been told.

The baby was wriggling around a little too much and the sonographer couldn't get all the measurements she needed. I tried turning, wriggling and star jumps to no avail. Never in any of my pregnancies had I had to get up and do star jumps in the examination room, and I felt like a right wally, but the sonographer assured me it happens all the time and sometimes it would jiggle baby in to a better position. Sadly, baby wouldn't budge though. The sonographer printed out some photos of the baby's hands, feet, face and body and an appointment was made for me to come back the following week to have an additional scan, so they could get the measurements they needed. I wasn't completely disappointed about this as the sonographer said everything looked great as far as she could tell, she didn't have any concerns, it was just that she couldn't get all the measurements so she couldn't be one hundred percent sure.

It meant I got another scan and another chance to see my baby boy! As before, my whole heart went out to the women who didn't have the same news and had to go through that scan alone.

Now we knew for certain our new person was a boy, we (my husband, children and I) went on a beautiful walk with the gender reveal cannon. It was silly and fun and my other two sons absolutely loved it and were insanely excited to be adding another little boy to their team. I got out my phone, videoed them setting off the canon (those things are tricky, aren't they?!) and captured the most magical rejoice in my husband and sons finding out they were going to have another son/brother. It was such a fun day and for a couple of hours we completely forgot the reality of the world we were living in. It was a lovely way of involving my husband and children in the pregnancy as this was really the first chance they'd had to do that.

Chapter Eight
The Rest of My Anomaly Scan

A week after my twenty-week anomaly scan, I went back to the hospital for a sonographer to get the measurements that they were unable to get the week before. I felt a lot less anxious this time. I had seen my baby on a screen three times now, there had been no cause for concern and the more you do something, the easier it becomes. I had gotten used to being on my own, handing over my notes and sitting down waiting for my name to be called out. So I sat, like before, behind my mask and notes in hand. I waited to be called in whilst my husband and children (sorry kids — I know this was so boring for you!) waited in the car.

I got called in, handed the sonographer my maternity notes and hopped on the bed. I tried my luck and asked if I would be able to record the baby for my husband to see, but was told no. I knew she'd say no, but decided it was worth asking. The sonographer was lovely, she put on the gel and turned the screen for me to see my little dancing baby. She immediately retrieved the measurements she needed and I cheekily asked if I could have another photo. She obliged and I left the room, beaming and relieved that the baby was developing as he should be and as healthy as expected.

This would be the last time I would get to see my baby, unless any additional scans were needed had there been any concerns, until the big day. It was bittersweet. I loved getting scans and being able to see my baby busting some moves, but the anxiety that comes with waiting to see if there is a heartbeat is something else, so I was pleased to have that part of the pregnancy over with, too.

Chapter Nine
What it Was Like Being Pregnant, in Public and in a Global Pandemic

THE prime minister announced that from 4th July 2020, pubs, restaurants and hairdressers could reopen, as long as they were Covid secure. This meant that risk assessments had been carried out, social distancing would be maintained, the workplaces would be well ventilated and everybody and everything was kept as clean as possible. Lockdown 1.0 was over and the country was able to resume some normality. For now, at least.

Naturally, people were simultaneously elated and petrified. At this point, it would still be a few weeks before face masks would become mandatory in shops and other indoor areas. I remember seeing people in other countries wearing them and I figured they may not help but they definitely couldn't hurt, so I took to my sewing machine and I made us all some. It turned out face masks did in fact help against the spread, which is why they were later introduced. My boys wanted some too and although children didn't have to wear them, they thought they were fun and would often wear them around the house whilst playing doctors and nurses.

Little did I know, shortly they would be available in all shops, petrol stations, you couldn't avoid them and they were as easy to get hold of as a loaf of bread. They had become mandatory in all public spaces, unless one had a valid, medical exemption. Seeing people wearing them on the streets went from strange to the norm, extremely quickly.

Our first outing post lockdown 1.0 was to the park at the end of our road. It had been closed since March and the kids were desperate to have a play. I was honestly terrified. I'd spent the entirety of my pregnancy keeping safe and essentially hidden from everybody and everything. Up until this day, the park had been sealed shut with yellow tape. All of a sudden, it was safe? As a mum, a pregnant person and just a person who had been told to stay at home to stay safe, the thought of being anywhere was terrifying. The phrase 'a walk in the park' had taken on a whole new meaning. The thought of going somewhere so simple certainly didn't feel like a walk in the park any more. It was incredibly odd and surreal. Particularly as different people had different views on the severity and importance of the rules.

I took the children to the park, but we all disinfected our hands with hand sanitiser first and I packed some with me to be used before and after each new piece of playground equipment. I hated what this was potentially doing to the boys but they didn't question it, they were just so happy to be allowed to go to the park. When we got there, it wasn't busy at all. I was so relieved. I still made them come to me for sanitiser before going on to the next piece of play equipment. They thought it was fun. My hand sanitiser smelt of strawberry laces and they loved smelling their hands afterwards. I was sure this incessant hand disinfecting would become old, but right now they found it novel and fun.

Soon after we arrived, more and more people came for a play. Astonishingly, I seemed to be the only person having an anxiety attack over anybody coming near my children and it turned in to a bit of a free-for-all, so I gathered up the boys and we came home for ice-cream instead. I'm sure I wasn't the only one panicking, it just felt that way. It was too much and my brain was having a hard time computing that it was now okay to mingle.

Social distancing still had to be maintained but little children couldn't be expected to do that and it was just a bit much right then. I had no idea what catching this virus would do to my children (born and in utero) and so I just wanted to hide, and the thought of going anywhere was filling me with dread.

The next few days we kept trying to go out, we felt guilt towards the children as they'd been locked up for so long. It was hard though. I was tying (so hard) not to let my fear show but I hated being out with every fibre of my being. I could actually see germs. Never in my life would I have referred to myself as a germophobe, but I was slowly becoming one. I kept talking to the baby in my tummy and saying how lucky they were to be kept safe and tucked away. In my naivety I hoped things would have settled down by the time the baby was born. I was convinced of it. And then my hormones would kick in, I would worry about the baby being born in the state of the world as it was and I would just sob. I wanted my little Pumpkin to stay safe and well forever.

The summer holidays were on the horizon which meant a break from remote-learning and a summer of just being outdoors as much as we could. We had a couple of socially distanced playdates planned (as much as you can enforce one of those with a two-year-old) and we would go strawberry picking, on picnics and to scarecrow festivals. Social distancing aside, it was easy to forget it wasn't just a normal July. We definitely did a lot more things with just us (we'd usually spend the summer in and out of friends' gardens, inviting people over and having paddling pool playdates) but when the sun shone, so did our moods.

Seeing, feeling and experiencing my ever-expanding tummy was wonderful. I found it so hard and sad not being able to share that with anybody though. Nobody got to awkwardly put their hands on my stomach and ask if I minded (I didn't, go ahead), nobody got to feel the flutters or kicks, nobody got to see me and ask if I was sure it wasn't twins, and nobody was able to celebrate this new growing life with me. It was amazing what things had been taken for granted before. I wanted that human interaction, I needed it.

One thing I found happening a lot, was people feeling the need to justify their movements and actions. It was so sad that people were having to do this but I think people were acutely aware that some people were ignoring the rules completely so they felt like they had to explain why they were seeing friends and family to others. Just to clarify that what they were doing was allowed. The whole situation was making people paranoid, jealous, sad and insecure. Never in my life would I imagine having to explain to somebody that seeing my family member was okay because it was legal, but here we were. For the most part, it wasn't allowed and that was just so much for people to get their head's around.

There were some caveats in the restrictions, which meant people could see other people. You could 'bubble' with families for childcare, if you lived alone and for some other reasons too. I would so often see people blatantly disregarding the rules and so would everybody else, which is why I think people felt they needed to justify it. I learnt to let it wash over me and not to worry what others got up to. It wasn't always easy but people would make their own choices and all I could do was focus on my little unit and make sure we were safe, well and doing everything we should.

The most infuriating and stressful thing to hear or witness was people comparing other people's stories. Like I wrote earlier, we were all in the same storm but very different boats. It was incredibly unhelpful and hurtful to hear 'at least you're not a first-time mum'. No. Just no. It was an ordeal for us all, let's be honest. Of course it was hard for first time mothers, but it was as hard for all pregnant women and mothers and this conversation around some having it harder than others was just unnecessary and unkind. If you were a first-time mum, you had the worry of not knowing what felt normal, if you should go and get checked out and just the general shine being taken from your pregnancy. If you had older kids at school, you had to deal with being pregnant in a pandemic whilst juggling home-schooling too. It absolutely wasn't a competition and at times it felt like the only people who could see this were pregnant women themselves. We would unite and empathise.

Hearing 'at least…' type comments was just not helpful.

Chapter Ten
The Summer of 2020

THE summer of 2020 was a memorable one. There were so many social restrictions, but in some ways, it was the most freeing time imaginable. Lockdown 1.0 was over, so most shops were now open and some social meetings were allowed, but social distancing still had to be maintained, the amount of people allowed to gather at once was limited and so many places were still shut.

Because of this, and the beautiful weather we had that year, it made for some really beautiful family days out. There was no rushing about, nowhere really to go, each weekend was just spent working out where else we could explore. We met up for strawberry picking and a socially distanced picnic one day with my parents, and once staying overnight at people's houses was allowed again, we took a few days in August to stay in Norfolk with my husband's parents. It was just all together a very slow and unwinding summer, most of which was spent lazing in the sun with my bump, cooling down with ice lollies.

There were still social restrictions which meant seeing friends, although not impossible, was considerably harder. But we managed a few playdates and we spoke to our neighbours over the fence and, as much as life was standing still right now, the weather was really helping us appreciate a simpler life.

Pregnancy-wise, this life suited me very well. I had severe sciatica at this point so I was thankful for the summer holidays which meant no school runs (had home schooling not been in place — they were a killer and I will always be grateful to my friend for doing all the ones she could to give my pain a break when the school runs would later start back up again), I could eat as many ice lollies as I liked and whilst I filled the paddling pool up for the children I would dangle my feet in and cool off. We bought a hammock for the garden that year, too. My pregnant self was very content and very relaxed, and my two sons were so happy just playing together with nowhere to rush to. I think that's one thing I will take from all the lockdowns, remembering there's really no need for all the rushing around we did pre-Covid. No guilt for not having anything planned, no over filling our weeks and cramming our diaries full of plans, no nothing. It was refreshing. Of course after a while it became boring and frustrating but with the glorious sunshine and a barbeque each weekend, it became a summer with heaps of positives.

We got to know our local area so well. We explored our local woods, beaches and villages. We entered our (socially distanced) village scarecrow festival and got to know so many members of our community. Woods, trees, grass, sand, nature! There was an abundance of it and we felt so fortunate to have it all so close by. At this point of the pandemic, we were allowed to travel for exercise. We would go on Google and hunt out some local woodland or a quiet beach that we'd not explored yet. We'd pack up a picnic and go exploring. My boys loved packing a backpack of treasures. Toy cars, a note pad, a toy figure. The rule was, if it fit in their bag, they could take it! We'd lather ourselves up in sun cream, put on a hat and we'd just explore. I would inevitably ask (make) Andrew to take a million bump shots and even more inevitably, Archie would insist he could take them better and make me do all sorts of silly and fun poses. We'd find rope swings, dens made out of sticks and would just plonk ourselves down and watch the kids play. I would instantly regret sitting on the floor as it practically took a crane to heave me back on to my feet, but it was all worth it. Every single blister, panting, back ache, sciatic pain (it really was agony, just awful), and whoever said pregnant people glowed rather than sweated clearly hadn't seen a pregnant woman in the height of summer doing nothing but walking day after day. Trust me. There was no glow. All sweat, baby.

There was anxiety leading up to September as everybody knew going back to school would be so different. We were told in emails what to expect. The children wouldn't need to wear facemasks but the teachers would in certain, communal areas. There would be stringent hand washing. Lunch times would be separated and staggered. As would play times. Children could only mix with other children in their bubble. It sounded so scary and unnatural. My son's school were great and had sent through a visual aid for the children to look at so they could see how the school would look when they got back and talked through all of the differences. We could go through this with our children so when it was time for them to go to school, it wouldn't be too much of a shock. Of course lots of children had still attended school over lockdown, those whose parents were keyworkers, and we had heard from them that all of the children had adapted so well and it wasn't so scary, so that was refreshing. But still it was so unknown and daunting and unnerving. It was an unprecedented time and we'd just spent months at home, safe. Protected. My health visitor asked how I was feeling emotionally about sending my eldest back to school so close to my due date. I said I was scared but knew he'd absolutely love being back with his friends, teachers and in a routine he loved. She mentioned if it was too much anxiety to mention it to the school and to see if keeping him off further was an option. I appreciated her support and understanding. I didn't end up talking to school about it. My husband worked between both hospitals. He had as much chance of bringing Covid home as my son did. We would just continue to do what we had been doing and keep as clean and safe as possible. We would make sure we would clean my son's entire uniform each day and just wash our hands as much as possible. I didn't want the summer to end, but I knew it was time and getting closer to September which meant we were only a month away from meeting our new baby and that was the best distraction from the scary reality that we could have asked for.

Chapter Eleven
Clapping for Our National Health Service

UNDOUBTEDLY, NHS workers were our heroes. Do you remember each Thursday evening clapping for them? Each Thursday, people would stand at their front doors and clap for two minutes. Some would play instruments or bang pots and pans. At the time I remember thinking, 'I've just got my kids to bed, please don't wake them!' but actually what a lovely community act to show our appreciation that was. Particularly as my husband was one of those heroes we were clapping for. I hated that he had to go to work in a hospital, I just wanted him to stay home and safe. But he carried on working as normal and I will be forever grateful to all the keyworker and frontline workers. They carried us through.

The appreciation and acknowledgment for our NHS was just wonderful. We really are so lucky to have such a wonderful health service available to us. The hospitals were swamped and staff were under enormous pressure. Keyworkers were faced with something unimaginable and kept on working tirelessly to keep us safe. They would have to work alongside patients with Covid, knowing they could contract it and bring it home to their own families. Clapping wasn't enough, and it would never change the situation, but it was a gesture to show our gratitude and I know so many staff really appreciated the boost. My husband used to laugh, as when it was time to clap, he'd often be arriving home from work, so he would drive down our road to people on their doorsteps clapping. It just made him giggle, and he remembers feeling awkward getting out the car not knowing how to be. Maybe he should have timed his home time better to avoid any awkwardness. Ha!

The symbol to spread hope and show solidarity during lockdown was a rainbow. People all over the country decorated the fronts of their houses in rainbows. It was a sign of unity and appreciation. I bought my children some window chalk paints and we painted a huge rainbow across our front window, with a message thanking the NHS. You couldn't walk out of your door without seeing rainbows. It was lovely. There were flags, paintings, posters. Rainbows had infiltrated houses, shops, schools, offices and hospitals and it was just a really beautiful thing.

People all around the country were selflessly and tirelessly fundraising for the NHS. Sir Captain Tom Moore was a British Army Officer. At the age of ninety-nine he began walking to raise funds. He would walk laps of his garden, his aim was to raise one thousand pounds by the time he turned one hundred. He got a lot of media attention and he smashed his target and actually raised over thirty million pounds by his one hundredth birthday. In total, he raised over thirty-two million pounds. How incredible. He was knighted by the Queen in what would be the palace's first socially distanced ceremony. He would sadly later die in hospital, from this awful disease.

Of course Captain Tom wasn't the only person to fund raise, adults and children nationwide wanted to use their time for something good. Another positive in what was a less than happy time. Community, coming together appreciation and thanks. It was a hard time but it's amazing what this country can do when it's on its knees. There were people who had to work on the frontline. Hospital workers, supermarket staff, teachers, emergency services, childcare workers, the armed forces, transport workers; the list is long and it isn't lost on me what those workers risked to keep the country going.

Chapter Twelve
Online Baby Shopping Just Isn't the Same!

OF course, in the midst of a global pandemic, baby clothes shopping is at the bottom of the list of things for people to worry about. However, you do get excited, don't you? It doesn't matter if it's your first or third or, I imagine, your tenth, imagining who they will be and going shopping with your friends/partner/mum and getting cute teeny tiny clothes is just part of the pregnancy process. All I can say is, thank goodness for Instagram small businesses and H&M's free delivery! I think not being able to go shopping for baby bits in itself was completely manageable but it was just another shadow casting over the current climate and reminding me how hard, and a bit pants, being pregnant right now was.

This pregnancy was my third baby and my third son, so I really didn't need a lot of stuff. We had a cot, we had enough clothes to dress a thousand babies and all the other essentials needed for a newborn. We didn't need anything. Aside from a new Moses basket mattress and nappies, I think we had everything else we needed. I can only imagine how much harder this aspect of expecting a baby must have been for first time parents who needed to start from scratch. What an amazing time we live in where we have everything at our fingertips though and a short scroll later we can order an entire nursery set. But still, it's not the same.

With my other two children, I would feel such joy in being in a supermarket and nipping to the clothes section to have a gander at some cute baby bits. Although supermarkets were still open throughout the pandemic, touching what you had no intention of buying was most definitely frowned upon. Looking at little baby clothes without touching and feeling them is nigh on impossible. The odd time that I did venture out, I just didn't want to particularly browse or buy anything for the baby. I wanted to get in and out as quickly as possible. I was struggling with the enormity of the situation and how serious it was. I could see germs. It wasn't a pleasant or exciting time to be shopping for a brand-new baby, so I didn't bother. I stuck to online instead. And once it had arrived, I'd put it straight in the wash.

Again, I was incredibly thankful for the times we were living in that buying online even was an option, but it just wasn't the same. It wasn't the same as going with your husband or your parents or your friends and choosing something really special and holding up a couple of outfits trying to decide which one to buy.

Just a week or two after we had found out I was pregnant, and just before the pandemic was announced, we had been to London for the weekend. We went in to a beautiful baby store in Kings Cross and my eldest asked if he could choose the baby a toy. He chose him a beautiful rhino rattle and it is now one of his very favourites. I will always look at that rhino and remember how special it is and how it is the only item we ever bought for the baby in person. If only we knew then what we did just a couple of weeks later. I don't think I'd have believed it.

Chapter Thirteen
Drive-By Baby Showers

I had a baby shower for my first baby in 2014, and it was wonderful. I didn't have one for my second in 2017 so I didn't feel like I needed or should have one for this baby. Lucky really, eh, as it was illegal to have anybody in your house at this point! However, part of me did want a little celebration, too. All of my friends and family (and the entire planet) were going through such a hard time and I would have loved to have drunk mocktails and play silly games whilst celebrating our new human. I didn't want any presents (what do you even need when pregnant with your third?!) but a get together with my favourite girls would have been ace.

It's okay that I didn't have one, I had a wonderful one with my first, but I do feel sad that I didn't have any choice. I think that's the kicker really, and what a lot of people struggled with through Covid, having the choice taken away. I was lucky though I'd already had a beautiful one years ago. So many pregnant mums (real life friends and online friends) did want a baby shower and the way they went around it was just lovely! Drive-by baby showers became a thing. At points during Covid, you were allowed people in your garden and then some in your house and then both and then neither. The rules changed a lot! When you were allowed people over, I know of people who had small gatherings in their garden, which was just lovely. But when this wasn't allowed, I saw mamas to be, have drive-by baby showers, and I remember thinking how fun and creative they were! The mum to be would sit in her front garden, whilst her 'guests' would slowly drive by her house in sort of a parade like fashion, blaring music and waving and honking. It was a far cry away from a traditional baby shower, but it was a lot of fun and it was making the most out of a bad situation. People celebrated birthdays like this too.

'Zoom' became very popular in 2020 also. The virtual meeting place. Baby showers became popular over Zoom too. You could get dressed to the nines, have your own mini buffet going on at home, and your girlfriends would all do the same in front of their laptops in their own living rooms. It was new, it was different, it was far from traditional but it was creative and fun and the only option really. The pandemic brought a huge sense of togetherness and community spirit and planned events such as baby showers really showed this.

Chapter Fourteen
Thankful for Friendships

I moved to East Yorkshire (from South Yorkshire, about an hour down the M62) when I got married in 2012. My husband is from Norfolk and had already moved here when he was offered a job in Hull, working between the two hospitals. Andrew had made friends thorough his work but I didn't know anybody. I got a job here just before I moved and through work, I formed friendships too. In 2015 we stayed in the area but moved to a different village, this is where I would continue to form more friendships, mainly thanks to my eldest son starting preschool and then school. I got to know other school mums who became great friends, I met friends through baby groups and I got to know my neighbours too. I am so incredibly thankful for my amazing friends. It is hard not having family to call in on without forward planning, as none of them live close, and here I have made friends for life who I know would be there for me and my family if and when we need anything.

When pregnant with this baby, I had friends offering to do school runs, to go shopping, left me flowers on my doorstep and were all together just a huge powerhouse of support throughout my entire pregnancy. They had their own families to support and guide through the pandemic but they still found and made time for me and my family and I am so incredibly grateful for that.

When newly pregnant, a friend who I knew reasonably well at that point but who soon became an incredibly special and important friend, came over as she had ordered some baby leggings from me and she said to save me posting them, she'd pop by. This was out of lockdown of course and at a point where you were allowed around each other's houses. I never make any assumptions so at that point hadn't considered who the cute little leggings could have been for. She came over and joyfully announced that she was expecting a baby and the order was for her! It was the most wonderful news. This would be her first baby and she and I were both overjoyed with her news. I hadn't had my first scan at that point but I couldn't keep it in, I had to tell her I was pregnant too! I didn't want to wait until my scan just to tell her over text a couple of weeks later, it felt natural to tell her now so we could celebrate together. We jumped up and down, began talking dates (my friend was due approximately a month before me) and just generally shared and rejoiced in each other's excitement.

From that point on, my friend and I would become incredibly close and were able to share this unique and petrifying experience together. We were both pregnant in utterly uncertain times and it was so refreshing having somebody who could relate. We would bounce thoughts and feelings off of each other and generally talk babies, pregnancy and all things pandemic.

We didn't know it just then, but that would be the last time we would see each other until just before my friend gave birth. There were lockdowns galore and we just didn't have the opportunity to get together. I am so thankful for text messaging, we couldn't see each other but we could still talk.

My friend popped by just before her baby came and although she wasn't allowed in, we were able to ask my husband to take a socially distanced bump shot in the front garden and we were able to wish each other well before she became a mama, and I became a mama again.

My friend's baby came, and then my baby came and we longed for nothing more but to meet each other's baby and give them all the cuddles. It wasn't allowed, so we settled for a doorstep meet-and-greet and planned on doing a baby class together, so we could spend time together and our babies could bond. Again, baby classes weren't allowed so sadly our friendship would have to continue via text message but we had plans to meet each other when we were allowed and to one day do a baby class together.

I am so incredibly grateful for every single one of my friends during this time. I wish I could have seen them and hugged them and shown them my new baby boy, but it wasn't to be. Their friendships never faltered and I will always be so incredibly thankful for their love and support and hope they know how much they mean to me.

Chapter Fifteen
The Virtual Midwife

OUR hospital (Hull Women and Children's) had an (in my opinion) invaluable service called 'Ask the Midwife'. It was a Facebook service with a senior midwife at the other end where in office hours you could send a message to the page and they would reply as soon as they could. In a time where pregnant mums had more questions and concerns than usual and fewer appointments than normal, having that extra support was incredible.

The first time I needed to use 'Ask the Midwife' was about my GBS diagnosis. I'd come off the phone call at my 16-week appointment and typically, I'd thought of everything I wanted to ask as soon as I'd hung up.

Google helped a little, but I wanted to speak to somebody and not just read forums. The midwife (angel) I spoke to was a lady called Jennifer. I must have sent her a million rambly (panicky) messages and she was so kind and reassuring the entire time. A real lifeline. My middle child was born with multiple allergies and there are some studies that suggest antibiotics in pregnancy and infanthood can disturb their gut microbiome and therefore contributing towards allergies. With this in mind, I had spent my entire pregnancy avoiding antibiotics. I had taken them for my initial UTI diagnosis but very reluctantly and only when telling the doctor of my concerns. Of course if I really needed them I wouldn't have put my own or my unborn baby's health at risk, but equally if I could avoid them, I wanted to. So when I read that to protect the baby contracting GBS in labour, I would need an antibiotic drip, I panicked. I went straight to Jennifer and told her my worries and concerns and she told me in detail exactly what my options were. She was extremely calm and reassuring and I'm so glad she was my virtual midwife.

After telling Jennifer I was allergic to penicillin (the antibiotic usually offered to GBS patients in labour) she told me plan B and the exact drug I would be offered, at what point it would be administered and how often I would need it. She went in to great detail and I came away really feeling like I had a plan and I could cope.

Instantly calm. At no point did she give me advice, but rather balanced views and clear options. I could either forego antibiotics in labour to avoid damaging the baby's gut but putting them at risk of contracting GBS or I could take the one dose (which we thought would be enough as it was my third labour and they usually get quicker) which would make my baby infinitely safer but potentially upset their tummy. I went for the latter option as I would take any potential allergies over an unimaginable alternative, but immediately started taking probiotics to offset any negative outcomes from having the antibiotics, and I got some in for when baby was born too. I ran my entire plan and verbalised all of my thoughts to Jennifer and she was completely helpful, all of the time.

Another time I had some excruciating pain in my ribs. Now, I'd been pregnant before. I knew what it felt to have a little foot stuck in or under the ribs. Agony. But this was in a different league. It took my breath away and reduced me to tears. It was worse at night when I tried to lay down. I tried sleeping sat up but I'd inevitably end up slouched in a heap and a crick in my neck, and the pain in the ribs would come back regardless. When the pain came, it was so painful that I couldn't just flip over and try a new position, I had to physically hold my rib, push and hold my breath. It really was so awful. I'd take labour over that any day.

Anyway, I decided to send Jennifer a message, venting about the pain and asking what I should do. Although I knew she couldn't diagnose me with anything over Facebook, it was so incredibly helpful to just talk through how I was feeling and ask for her advice. She told me to come to the hospital and a few hours later I was diagnosed with Costochondritis. There wasn't anything I could do besides take paracetamol (as other drugs which they would usually prescribe couldn't be taken in pregnancy) but having the option to talk it through really helped. If that service wasn't there, I probably wouldn't have seen anybody about it as I didn't have a regular midwife who I could contact and we all know how long GP surgeries take to get through to. So again, I was very grateful to Jennifer and the Facebook service and I do hope they keep it going after the pandemic as it could be a lifeline for a lot of expectant mums.

Chapter Sixteen
Lone Appointments

WHEN I was diagnosed with Costochondritis, I was sent to the maternity day unit to wait my turn and be assessed. It's where pregnant ladies were sent for any concerns including any unusual symptoms or reduced foetal movement. Everybody had to attend these appointments alone. Except they weren't really appointments, you just had to take a seat and you'd be called in, in order of urgency. With my ribs, I wasn't worried about the baby. I was there for my own health so I wasn't particularly anxious or worried that I had to be alone.

However, there were so many women there that I am sure would have been there for reduced movements therefore feeling much more anxious. With my other two children, I experienced reduced movement with both (miraculously I never did with this one, so I didn't need to go through the worry of sitting and waiting to be monitored). When foetal movements change, the advice is you should go to the hospital to be assessed by a midwife. With both of my older children I remember the long wait. The wait in the waiting room to be triaged and then further waiting until they put you and your baby on a machine to monitor movements. It was long, worrying and anxiety inducing. The times I went in with my other sons, I at least had my husband with me. I was just as scared, but I wasn't alone. The midwives are always fantastic and so thorough, but it is a long wait until they are happy baby is moving as they should (even though typically as soon as you turn up, they start doing cartwheels in your uterus and use your bladder as a trampoline) and I can only imagine how petrifying doing that wait on your own is.

Some appointments didn't really bother me that I was alone as there was a lot of waiting around, a bit of urine admin and then if we were lucky, a listen of baby's heartbeat (which I would always record on my phone to show my husband). It was the bigger appointments that felt unfair that we needed to go to them alone. The scans, the appointments later on when I was in pain and could have done with some physical support as well as emotional. I was one of the lucky ones though. It was women who had previous losses I felt for, or those with high-risk pregnancies. We all knew it was to keep us safe, but it was hard to go through it alone, particularly when you could meet at restaurants and pubs over the summer (remember 'Eat Out to Help Out'?), but you couldn't have your partner, friend or mum come with you to take you to a maternity appointment.

When I was pregnant with my first son, I went with my husband on a course of antenatal classes. They prepared us with what to expect in labour, they taught us different terms that may be used and showed us various birthing equipment. The classes covered feeding, the newborn days and were ran by a midwife who answered as many questions as possible. I didn't need these classes for my second or third son, but I found them incredibly invaluable with my first. These classes were still taking place throughout the pandemic, but like everything else, they were now online. It was great that the organisers were still making it possible to access them, but it must have felt unfair to the parents-to-be that they couldn't have the face-to-face class. Not everybody enjoys online sessions, they can be a bit awkward and just aren't as immersive. This is nobody's fault, it's just lack of human interaction. I imagine attendance of antenatal classes were a lot lower in 2020 because of this. They're not essential of course, but they are fun to go to and a part of the lead up to welcoming your new baby. They are great for any questions you have and can help make new friendships and connections too. It's just another experience Covid stole from expectant parents.

I found it incredibly unfair that you were unable to record any part of your scan. It was hard enough that we were made to go alone. It wasn't as if we were asking to record the whole thing or set up a live stream, just to be given ten seconds after the sonographer had done their job, to be able to document it to show our partners. It was up to each individual trust to decide if it was something they would allow. We (pregnant women) weren't asking a lot. It was our information, our data.

We would have just been asking for ten seconds at the end of our scan to use our phone to record the baby wriggling, so we could take it home and show our partners what they would have seen had they been allowed in.

Lone appointments extend to the rules surrounding labour. At this point, if you had your baby in hospital, you had to go in on your own until you were in established labour, which is 4cm dilated. This inevitably meant some women would have had to labour alone. Not everybody drives, it wouldn't have been the case for everybody for the labouring woman to go in to hospital and their partner to wait in the car (like Andrew had planned to do). Some will have had to get taxis or ambulances, were there partners supposed to wait in the car park or the foyer of the hospital until they were allowed up to delivery? That could have taken hours. The rules were terribly frustrating. I kept trying to understand why rules were put in place and try to see the government's point of view, but it was very hard at times like this.

If a labour progressed quickly and the woman's birthing partner were unable to get there in time, it will have meant they missed out on the birth. I could understand so many of the new Covid rules, but having the women labour alone was not one of them. If the woman was admitted, their birthing partner should have been able to be there, too.

Giving birth can be terrifying. As lovely and kind as the midwifery team are, you want your birthing partner there. Most of the time, your birthing partner will live with you so I found little sense in them not being allowed in the delivery room with you the entire time. There would still be the same number of potential risk/germs so I'm not sure why after a lonely pregnancy, they were insistent on you getting to the finish line partly alone too. It was a really, really strange time. I always said if I went to the pub I could have laboured with my husband and a whole room of strangers. I appreciate they wanted as few people in a hospital as possible to stop the spread of Covid but to labour alone wasn't fair, especially as your partner was allowed in eventually anyway.

Chapter Seventeen
Pumpkins and a Photoshoot

SINCE the day I found out I was pregnant and worked out my due date to be slap bang in the middle of my favourite month, I knew I wanted to save for a proper maternity photoshoot, outdoors, surrounded by pumpkins. I'd never had a maternity shoot before and my obsession with pumpkins borders on unhealthy so as soon as we started telling people I was expecting, I booked my incredibly talented photographer friend for a shoot. I adore being pregnant, I'm always huge (I have really long babies!) and always in so much discomfort but the way it makes me feel is ten to none. It is so incredibly special and I wanted to capture it and remember it forever.

I emailed my local pumpkin patch and said I knew it was months and months away but would it be okay if I used their pumpkin patch for our shoot. We even discussed the best date to choose with how green or orange the field would be. A lot of preparation went in to this photoshoot! The owners of the pumpkin patch we chose were incredibly helpful and humoured me when I began emailing them in May (I am incredibly organised okay, this isn't even weird to me) and would even send me photos of field updates to show me how orange the pumpkins were looking. Naively, we all assumed Covid would have 'settled' by then, or at least the current restrictions would be a thing of the past.

Luckily, the photoshoot went ahead as it was outside and we weren't in lockdown at that point so we were able to travel for things that weren't considered essential, but we were so close to it not being allowed. My (photographer) friend and I were texting the week before (as it all changed daily) discussing different options if it couldn't go ahead. I would have been heartbroken if I'd have had to cancel and I imagine there were so many, less lucky, parents in this situation. You save, you plan, you choose your outfit. It's a now or never type situation too because you want to capture your bump in all its glory but you can't leave it too long otherwise there will be no bump to photograph!

Anyway, the shoot went ahead and we made some incredible memories to treasure for a life time. It was muddy, my just-turned three-year-old fell over and got dirty knees before we'd even began, but it was incredibly fun. We just had a walk in the field and watched the sun go down and got some great bump shots and some great family shots. I absolutely adore being pregnant (sickness and pain aside) and having a big baby bump is my favourite so being able to capture so many images of my pregnant state was wonderful. I know not everybody got to do that and I'm sorry if you were one of those who had to cancel such a special time in your pregnancy.

I photograph everything. I capture everything. It's my hobby and my passion and I am unapologetic when it comes to doing so, so having a professional document my bump was so incredibly important and special to me and I'm so grateful that we narrowly avoided having to cancel it. Here's hoping I can return to the field for a first birthday pumpkin shoot.

Chapter Eighteen
The Tier System

ON 14th October 2020, the day before I was due to give birth, a tier system was introduced across England. See, even at this point we had no idea what the rules and law would be surrounding visitors. We really had no idea how to proceed until the baby was actually here. Rules were constantly changing and it was sometimes hard to keep up!

There were three tiers; medium, high and very high. Depending on where you lived and what tier your area had been assigned depended what restrictions had been lifted. East Riding was in tier two (high) which meant you couldn't mix households indoors, and when outdoors you were limited to meeting as a group of six. The hospitality sector remained open but with restrictions and a curfew. My mum had temporarily moved in with us that week to be our childcare for when I went in to labour, and after checking she was still allowed to be here (she was) our lives didn't really change. We asked her to stay with us this time as opposed to texting her when labour began like last time, because of the GBS.

We had to go into hospital at the first sign of labour and my parents live an hour away, so we needed to have her a lot closer, so she moved in for a while whilst we waited for the baby's arrival. We stayed on baby watch and our lives were very much the same as before the tier system came in. I was too big and too sore to socialise even if I wanted to and soft play remained open in tier two, so me and mum could take Rory there whilst we sat and waited for the new little person to arrive. In all honesty, the thought of soft play (all those germs!) was terrifying but Rory needed it, we needed a change of scenery and our lovely, local one is small and clean and we felt very safe. My mum and I sat on the sofa and ordered drinks and snacks, whilst Rory went down the slide (his favourite) a million times. Adults had to wear masks in soft play but only when walking around, so whilst we sat and watched Rory play we didn't need to wear them and could just enjoy watching him be three. There'd been so much the children had missed out on recently, so watching him do something very normal was just lovely. I didn't know at the time, but this would be the last time in a very long time that we would be able to go to soft play. Something I didn't think I would ever miss! But I did, massively.

I spent the 'tier days' up until labour just like lockdown really, aside from the trip to soft play and a hobble around the shops, we just sat indoors and nested. My mum did the jobs that always need doing but you never find time for. She organised our kitchen cupboards and I couldn't have been more grateful! She embraced and joined in my crazy, nesting frenzy and helped me tidy up after my three-year-old hurricane, I was so grateful she was there to help not only with the childcare when I was in labour but to keep me company the week before. So, tier system or no tier system, I had already created my own little cocoon of solitude so it didn't bother me so much. My husband was at work as normal, my eldest son at school and my amazing friend who has a son in my son's class offered to bring him home a couple of times a week for me so

I didn't need to struggle. I will always be so grateful for that and Archie had so much fun and absolutely loved the days she was picking him up! So, we just plodded along and waited. And waited and waited. Archie and Rory both went over their expected due date so I wasn't expecting to go in to labour with this one anytime soon. I used this week to really enjoy a quiet pace of life and spend time with my mum. We don't live close enough to pop in for a cuppa (pre-Covid times when that was allowed) so spending a week with her like this was really lovely.

Chapter Nineteen
My Final Antenatal Appointment

I was forty weeks (plus four days) pregnant and on my way to what would be my final midwife appointment. I had a hopeful feeling that this would be the last one and took plenty of bump selfies before I headed off. I jumped (read hobbled/flopped) in the car and drove to the children's centre in the village.

Whilst I sat waiting to be called, I remember rubbing my stomach wondering if this would be my last appointment before meeting my baby. There was one other woman waiting and she looked almost ready to meet her baby too, I wondered if this would be her last appointment also.

My name was called, I took what felt like an age to get on my feet, and followed the midwife. We went in to the room and I handed her my notes. She handed me a urine sample pot and asked me to go to the bathroom.

Embarrassingly, I couldn't see what I was doing thanks to my humongous bump and I completely missed. I tried again, but there was nothing left so I sheepishly returned to the midwife with an empty pot. Oh, the shame! The midwife chuckled, said it happened all the time, and suggested we get through the rest of the appointment and I could try and go again at the end.

It was a fairly quick appointment. I hopped on the bed and my bump was measured. I had been told throughout most of the pregnancy that I was measuring big, but not too big so there was no concern. I felt huge! My bump size was plotted on a graph and it was following the curve nicely. I knew he wouldn't be a small baby considering the weights of my other two and considering my current mammoth size!

The midwife listened to the baby's heartbeat and offered me a stretch and sweep. This process would involve her checking my cervix and encouraging it to separate from the membranes of the amniotic sac and I agreed she could give it a go. It was painless and quick. She said it was successful and to expect to go in to labour quite quickly. I was excited but hadn't pinned my hopes on labour starting too soon. I was hopeful and optimistic, but just waited to see what would happen. She listened to the baby's heartbeat again to make sure he was happy (he was) and I got off the bed.

It was time to try and pee in a pot again! Thankfully, this time it was a lot more successful. I didn't miss, the midwife was able to check my urine, and I was fine. I went home and eagerly awaited labour and wondered if it would be happening anytime soon.

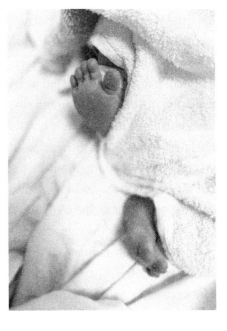

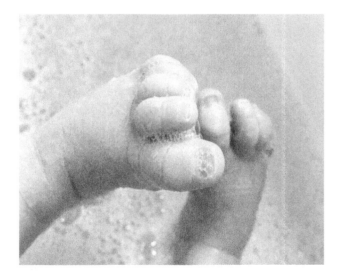

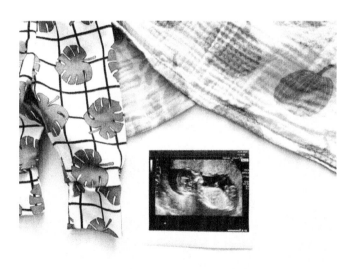

Part Two:
Labour

Chapter Twenty
Labour

I went in to labour on 20th October 2020. I was five days overdue (I had gone overdue with my other two babies so this came as no surprise). The day before, I had been to see the midwife who told me it would be any day and to go on a walk and bounce on my birthing ball. My sciatica was almost unbearable at that point so a walk was out, but I did go home and bounce on my birthing ball. I then had a warm bubble bath loaded with clary sage and when my biggest boy got home from school that day, I got him ready for his swimming lesson. My husband would be taking Archie to his swimming lesson, and as Andrew was the one who would also need to drive me to the hospital and I would need to go in straight away, we did waver slightly on whether he should go in case Archie was underwater when I went in to labour, but we decided as the pool was close and I had no indication that labour was imminent, it would be fine. They went and I cooked spaghetti and meatballs for dinner whilst my mum played with Rory. It was all very normal and I had no indication that labour would be starting relatively soon. Aside from the fact he was fully cooked and ready to be born.

Whilst my mum was staying with us, it had become a bit of our routine that we would watch 'The Cube' in an evening and I would sit and get some bouncing in.

Archie was home from swimming, we'd eaten our spaghetti and meatballs and the kids had been bathed and were asleep in bed. So there I sat, bouncing and chatting (yelling at the TV) about how we would have done the challenges differently.

I went to bed as normal, slept as normal (up a million times to pee and couldn't get comfy so all in all pretty terribly) and at around seven o'clock the next morning my eldest came in to wake us up for school. Archie is always the first awake in our house and he is always our little wake up call. I remember sitting up in bed and immediately wondering if I'd wet myself or my waters had gone. There was no pain and no movie-like gush and this wasn't how they'd gone in previous pregnancies. (In my first pregnancy I was induced and my waters were broken for me and with my second the waters went just as I started to push). I casually sauntered to the toilet to investigate further and realised it was most probably my waters and actually I hadn't wet myself. Neither would have been a surprise to be honest but I was confident that I was in labour and it was time to meet my baby.

It was only me and Archie awake and there was something really exciting about us having our own little secret. I told him that the baby was coming and that mummy had to get ready and that Nana would be looking after him. I decided to quickly straighten my hair and put on a little make up (there's something about looking your best equalling feeling your best). I grabbed my bag with my mask (pandemic life), hospital notes and a few other basics and woke up my husband.* I think he would agree that my calmness in these

---

* Although I had packed two hospital bags already (one for myself

situations always make him panic more, so I left him to snooze whilst I got some clothes out for the big two to wear and finished getting myself ready. I was being quick but also making sure we were all ready and I hadn't forgotten anything in a panic. I gently roused Andrew and whilst he was getting ready, I woke my mum. Rory woke up too and was a little confused with the commotion and I remember perching on the bed, cuddling and rocking him just like I did with his big brother when I was in labour with him.

My waters continued to trickle so we put a towel down in the car and I phoned the hospital whilst we were on our way to tell them I was coming in. I told them I had GBS which is why I was coming so early and they said they'd be waiting for me and would see me soon. On the phone to the hospital, I got my first contraction and I knew it wouldn't be long before I was in full blown labour. My first contraction wasn't too painful, but it was painful enough that I knew I was in labour and it made me incredibly giddy and excited. I was just raring to get to the hospital and meet my new person.

We were prepared for my husband to need to wait in the car but the contractions were getting stronger and I think in the moment we forgot about the 4cm rule. I had a big and painful

---

and one for the baby), I packed a third, very small and basic bag. We had no idea at what point my husband would be able to come in to the hospital with me and although useful for many other things, at that point my husband was very much needed to carry his labouring, pregnant wife's bags in to hospital. I decided to pack a tote bag with notes, a charger, my purse and underwear, which I could carry up on my own and then my husband could bring up the main bags from the car when I called him to say he was allowed up. At that time, the hospitals insisted on you labouring alone until you reached 'active labour' which is 4cm dilated.

contraction in the car park, so I took a few moments to let it pass and we went straight to the delivery suite where I was assessed and as I was in active labour already, there was no need for my husband to leave. He had to wear his mask throughout, but thankfully I did not.

This is where all of my anxieties about giving birth in the middle of a global pandemic could potentially come to fruition. This is the point that my baby would be born in to a germy hospital and not be protected by me, where if anything happened to me or the baby, my husband would be unable to stay with us. Where things just became very real. Adrenaline is a wonderful thing though. All of these anxieties were kept at bay and I was able to concentrate on the task at hand. I didn't really have time to worry about anything but the pain and getting my baby out safely.

I actually remember feeling very calm and that was thanks to my husband knowing how I wanted my space (things to stimulate and work with all five senses; lavender spray to smell, photos of my children to see and music to listen to, he brushed my hair and made sure I had enough to drink) and my incredible midwife, Michelle. She was completely led by me and I felt completely empowered in an otherwise helpless and vulnerable situation. She noticed on my hospital notes that I was due to give birth in the MLU (midwife led unit) and she didn't tell me I couldn't go in there, but she told me the MLU wouldn't be too different to the room I was currently in. It was great, it was huge and there was a sofa and a birthing ball and aside from it not having dim lighting which I was hoping for, it was perfect. Michelle turned the main light off but put the side and bathroom lights on so it actually ended up being dim, cosy and I felt more than happy there. I had to wait for the doctor anyway (for my GBS antibiotics) and we didn't think it would be long before baby was here, so I chose to stay put.

Michelle went to find a doctor to put in my cannula so he could start administering the antibiotics, to get them in to my system in time to protect the baby. Whilst she was away, I perched on the bed whilst Andrew found me a nightie to change into, and made sure everything we needed for the baby was to hand. I went in to the adjoining bathroom, got in to my nightie (pink with white hearts and buttons down the middle), put my hair in a top knot and made sure I was as ready as I could be for the main event. My waters were steadily leaking at this point and my contractions were ramping up. I was excited! I sat on the edge of the bath in the bathroom and held on to the support rail as another contraction came and went, then I walked back to the bed and waited for the doctor. Andrew turned off the radio that was playing and brought out our iPad and, at my request, put on Fleetwood Mac. I had listened to them a lot in my pregnancy and they were my band of choice at that point. They were familiar and made me feel comfortable and calm. Andrew had made me a specific labour playlist but I planned on saving that for later.

The doctor arrived, ready to put in my cannula. He asked if I had a preference to which hand it was put into, so I offered up my left. He had read my notes and seen my 'allergic to penicillin wrist band' that Michelle had given me, but I double checked that he was giving me an alternative antibiotic (clindamycin) which he was. It didn't hurt, I don't really remember him putting it in, I was too distracted. I do remember it bleeding quite a bit though and him apologising whilst Andrew cleaned me up with a baby wipe, ha! The blood had ended up on my feet as I was sat crossed legged on the bed, so I was a bit of a mess. But it was in, it didn't hurt, and the intravenous antibiotics were doing their job. They would go straight in to my system so when baby was on his way out, he would have protection against GBS. We just needed baby to stay put for a few hours whilst the antibiotics got to work. Thankfully he did.

I had never written a birth plan in any of my pregnancies. I always knew what I didn't want, but I really didn't mind how things went and was happy to just trust the process. This time however, I had learnt from my previous two experiences a couple of things I'd rather avoid and I felt like the current situation had taken away so much choice and I wanted a little bit of control back. I wrote a list and labelled it 'birth wishes'. We all know that there are no plans in childbirth, the baby will come when and how they are ready and you must prepare for all scenarios. My birth wishes simply stated the environment I would like to labour in, how I would like things to happen after he was born (skin to skin, breastfed and delayed cord clamping) and imperatively, how I wished to labour. I didn't want to be offered pain relief, I didn't want to be coached to push, I didn't want to lay down to push and I essentially wanted to be left to my own devices and I'd ask (or scream) for help if I needed it. Michelle listened to every single point on my list and actually thanked me for what I'd written. She was really so lovely and I'm so glad she was on shift that day.

I found myself comfiest, during contractions, bouncing along on the birthing ball. So I set that up in the corner of the room, next to the sofa. Andrew sat on the sofa, I bounced, wriggled and jiggled and he was at the perfect height for me to squeeze his knee when it got to the intense bit. We had battery operated tea lights on the window sill, Gilmore Girls on the iPad (I laboured to season one, episode twenty FYI) and in between contractions it was actually really lovely. We would just chat about what we thought our other children were up to, Andrew would load me up with sweets and a drink and we would watch the iPad whilst trying to remember positive birth affirmations and reminding myself to breathe.

The only strange/sad/noticeable bit that we were doing this though a global pandemic was that my husband had to wear a facemask for the duration. I was exempt (thankfully) but whilst my husband was with me, he had to wear a mask. It probably did a good job of hiding his grimaced face as I squeezed his knee through the pain of the contractions! He wasn't bothered, he was used to wearing a mask in hospital for his work day so it was nothing new. The midwifery staff and doctors were in full PPE too but aside from that, which you didn't really notice after a while, it was no different than giving birth in normal circumstances.

Most of my labour was done like this. Gilmore Girls, Lucozade, knee squeezing and smelling/smushing my eldest son's muslin in to my face, that I had sprayed in lavender spray. It calmed me down so much and there was something about being plunged in to darkness with an overwhelming hit of lavender that made the contractions much more bearable. Michelle would nip in and out and it was all very calm. There was my unborn baby's cot, ready and waiting for him for when he came earth side. My husband chose a vest (one that I had designed, with 'Little Pumpkin' adorned on it), baby grow (a brown, woodland one) and hat (one with pumpkins on, that I had made for him) for him to wear, got a tiny little nappy ready and positioned Maple (his bunny) in the corner of the cot, ready to be given to our baby as his first cuddly toy. Maple (or

Maples rather) will always be very special in our family. When I was pregnant with my first son in 2014, I bought him a bunny that I decided I wanted to be his first ever teddy and that it would come with me to the hospital and would wait in the little cot ready for his arrival. The bunny didn't have a name until I was in hospital, waiting for my induction to work, and I decided we should give it one. I was staying on Maple Ward, which is the antenatal ward for women needing specialist attention, such as inductions. We saw the sign stating Maple Ward and my husband and I decided to name the bunny Maple. Maple was my son's first teddy and he is so very loved.

When I was pregnant with my second son, I noticed that this exact bunny was still being sold so I bought one for him too. I actually bought two. We thought if we were lucky enough to have three children, they could all have the same bunny. They could all have a Maple. We thought it would be so lovely for them to have the same first teddy. It had become a little tradition and all three Maples are their favourite soft toys. It's very lovely. And hopefully one day, when they're big and grown, they will smile at the fact that they all have the same, very special, first teddy bear and that their mum was bonkers enough to buy Sonny's when she was pregnant with Rory, to make sure they could all have the same one.

A few hours passed and I knew baby was close. I remember saying this to Andrew and Michelle and I was put on the monitor. The monitor and my contractions suggested I wasn't as close as I felt, as my contractions were too far apart and not massively long. Michelle suggested I get back on the bed and she would examine me, but as soon as I got on the bed, I remember telling them he was coming. I wanted to be up right so I got tall on my knees and held on to the head rest of the bed. Somehow, in turning to face the head rest I pulled out my cannula. It didn't hurt, the adrenaline masked all of that, but it bled! A second midwife, who had just been called in, managed to pop it back in. This was at twelve-seventeen p.m. At twelve-thirty-one p.m I was holding 10lb 2oz of screaming, pink and precious newborn scrumptiousness. He was born to Led Zeppelin's 'Whole Lotta Love' and all worries and stresses of giving birth in these awful circumstances had fizzled away. I didn't notice who had masks on and had no idea what was going on in the outside world. We were instantly in our newborn baby bubble and it was perfect. Whilst in that room, it was perfect.

The pushing stage of labour came and went so, so quickly. One minute I was telling Michelle and Andrew that the baby was coming, then I accidentally yanked my cannula out and then it was instantly calm. I remember having a very slight panic and told the room that I couldn't do it. Michelle and Andrew quite rightly told me that I could and I would, and made me feel instantaneously calm and strong. I wasn't once told to push. I knelt up high, waited for my contraction and pushed and breathed. I heard one of the midwives say they could see some gorgeous hair and at that, his head was born and he let out the cutest and loudest cry. Only his head had been born but he was showing us all his lung capabilities and letting the world know he had arrived. I had a few seconds to catch my breath and I remember asking Andrew if that crying was our baby (I was in disbelief!) and then another push and he was here. We named him Sonny Stanley and we were totally and utterly in love with him. Because I was facing backwards, and on my knees, and the baby was still attached by his umbilical cord to my placenta which I hadn't birthed yet, we had to carefully manoeuvre him and me so I could turn, sit comfortably and cradle him.

In doing so, I managed to pull the cannula out (again!) but it wasn't needed this time so I left it out, got comfortable and offered the baby his first ever breastfeed. He took to it wonderfully and I just sat on the bed, in awe at this beautiful new creation, whilst waiting for my placenta to come. I wanted there to be a delay in clamping his cord, to make sure he had all his nutrients and goodness from the placenta. When it had stopped pulsing, Andrew cut the cord. The baby was weighed and given his vitamin K injection (to prevent a bleeding disorder called Haemorrhagic Disease of the Newborn) and he was handed back to me for cuddles.

I was then told, as he was my third baby, I was at higher risk of blood clots so I would be given Fragmin injections to administer myself at home, for ten days. I was given one there and then and shown how to do it and I was told I'd be given them, and a small sharps bin to dispose of the injections, before I was discharged.

The midwives and midwifery assistants came and gushed and congratulated us and I felt so strong, empowered and special. I felt like I could do anything. Oxytocin is a wonderful thing, I had never felt so good. We Face Timed family, took a million photos and I managed a shower and to give them enough pee eventually (if you know you know). About an hour after he was born, I think my body went in to a bit of shock. I went all cold and shivery and felt a bit strange. I was fine, the midwives got me some food and drink (how incredible is that first bite of toast after giving birth though?) and I just curled up in bed and watched my husband cradle my son. Having a snooze would have been logical at this point but I was so full of adrenaline and awe, I just couldn't. My body finally caught up with what had just happened and I felt much better.

Sometime later (we had to wait for a bed to become free on the postnatal ward), the porter came for me and Sonny which meant Andrew had to now go home. We all went in the lift together but Sonny and I had to get out first, whilst Andrew had to get out on a different floor, so it was a quick kiss and cuddle goodbye whilst the porter held the lift door open, and Sonny and I were taken by the porter and Suzanna (the loveliest midwifery assistant) to the postnatal ward. The porter dropped me at my bay, Suzanna took my bags and got me all settled in whilst I carried Sonny. It was at that point that I decided to route around my bag thanking past me for packing such excellent post birth snacks and to grab my phone and respond to messages and to take a copious number of photos of my brand-new baby.

The postnatal ward, as lovely as the staff were, was where being without a birthing partner was most noticeable. I don't want to say 'alone' because of course I had my little Sonny, and as soon as any midwifery staff were available, they would of course have helped me, but also — I *was* alone. I was sore and tired and it sucked. The midwifery staff were run off their feet so I wouldn't and couldn't buzz them unless I really needed them. I was terrified of leaving Sonny and just remember needing a wee and holding it in. My husband should have been there to hold our baby whist I went to the bathroom or had a shower. Instead, I forwent having any more showers (I knew I'd be home before long so could wait) and only when I was fit to burst would I run down the corridor to the toilet. I hadn't met my bay buddy at this point (she was *so* lovely) so I had no idea who was at the other side of my curtain and I was so stressed at leaving a tiny newborn who had only ever known me, my sound, my heartbeat for the last nine months, alone with a ward full of strangers. It was horrible. Had I been allowed to carry him outside of the bay, I would have taken him to the toilet with me. That, for me, was the hardest part of not being allowed any visitors.

Sonny and I were both medically well, and there was no reason I couldn't have gone home. However, because I had GBS, we needed to be monitored a little longer and have a few extra observations to make sure Sonny hadn't contracted it (he hadn't). The way the timings fell however, meant my husband couldn't visit at all. That wasn't great, honestly. Especially when I could hear through the other side of the curtain, my lovely neighbour have her partner visit for an hour. I heard her leave him with the baby whilst she went to the toilet and remember thinking that's probably the strangest thing I've ever been jealous of!

Our hospital's policy was, for every full day you're on the postnatal ward, your nominated birth partner can visit for one hour. Because I gave birth at lunch time on the Tuesday and was discharged on the Wednesday evening, there wasn't a full day in between which meant I wasn't allowed a visitor. Sure, it was great that I only had to stay in a day, and I never minded my husband not being able to be there the entire time, but I would have really appreciated just an hour visit so I could reset. You are so physically exposed as a new mother and are completely vulnerable. I would be feeding and the catering staff would just come in, the hearing test people couldn't get a true reading so had to come in and out a few times, I just really needed an advocate to talk to staff coming in and out, or somebody to hold Sonny whilst I slept (I didn't close my eyes once by the way, I couldn't) or somebody to throw a towel over me when I needed a bit of privacy. I felt vulnerable and exposed. That wasn't down to anybody in particular, just the dire situation.

I met my bay buddy the next morning and she was so lovely. I so wish we had exchanged details. She gave me her name but I'm ashamed to say that my adrenaline was responsible for me forgetting this. She overheard a conversation between myself and the catering staff. At that time, I had a dairy free diet. My second son has many allergies and I had decided to ensure there was no dairy in my breastmilk for the new babe. Had Sonny had a dairy allergy, by me having milk sans dairy would give his little belly a chance and I would know if any potential symptoms I had to look out for were normal newborn things (newborn rashes etc) or allergy symptoms.

Anyway, when the catering staff member came around with the menu, I asked if she had any dairy free options. She was less than helpful and I just told her it was fine, I had snacks and I'd just have a drink. She offered me tea or coffee and I asked if I could have something cold. Squash, water. I honestly don't think I was asking that much. I said please, I was polite. She wasn't happy, she walked away and I heard her talk about me to her colleague. Queue the new mum behind my curtain asking if she could come 'in'. She said she'd heard our conversation and she had made me a food package! She was vegan and said the previous day she had the same conversation and was met with the same level of unhelpfulness so her partner had brought in a load of safe snacks for her. This wonderful and beautiful human took it upon herself to fill a tub up with dairy free chocolate, snacks, safe butter, safe milk, biscuits- the list is endless. I thanked her and later on cried the hugest happy tears. If you've had a baby, you know how hungry you are afterwards and you just want to eat anything and everything. This kind lady got it and did the kindest thing and I will never forget that, always be grateful and in the most miniscule chance you are reading this, thank you. Thank you so much.

All the usual new baby admin was done, tests, checks, observations. Sonny was absolutely fine, as was I, so then we just had to wait for my Fragmin injections and be reminded how to use them, then we were discharged. I phoned my husband, said goodbye to my bay buddy and the porter came to wheel Sonny and I downstairs. As I wasn't a patient any more, the midwife had to insist that I wear a facemask whilst on my way out of the hospital. I had packed one just in case but thankfully I didn't need to rummage around my bags, the midwives gave me a disposable one.

My husband couldn't come to the ward or even the door, he had to wait downstairs. The lovely porter put my bags on the back of my wheelchair and we headed to the café next to the exit/entrance of the hospital. That's where Andrew and Archie were waiting for me. Sonny and I had been discharged at the same time that Archie had finished school, so Andrew picked him up first and they both came straight to the hospital to pick us up. The porter wheeled us through the winding corridors of the hospital and took us downstairs in the lift. He pushed us around the corner where we saw Andrew and Archie, eagerly awaiting our arrival. Archie jumped up with glee, so excited to meet his new brother. He stroked him, said hello, and gave me the biggest cuddle. He kept saying that he couldn't believe I'd had a baby, over and over again. I gave

Sonny to my husband to put in to his car seat and we went to the car to begin our life as a family of five.

Sonny became grizzly in his car seat and Archie spent the entire journey holding his little hand and singing to him.

The noticeable differences of giving birth in the current climate was the lack of, well, anybody. My mum was at home when we arrived there with Sonny, as she was looking after my other children whilst I was in labour. When I phoned to say I was being discharged, my dad drove from Doncaster to pick up my mum. So thankfully they both got to meet Sonny, but they left shortly after a quick cuddle and a few photographs as they wanted us to settle in to our new family. At the time of writing, they are the only people that have been able to properly meet Sonny. There have been doorstop hellos, school run coos and Face Times from people, but this has been his one and only meeting. It's really sad.

The first meeting between the three brothers was absolutely gorgeous though and a moment ingrained in to my memory. Archie had met Sonny already, so when the four of us walked through the door to see Rory and my parents, he was just full of pride. Andrew put Sonny, who was in his car seat, on the floor in the middle of the living room and his brothers crouched down beside him. Archie held his hand and Rory stroked his face. Rory kept saying how cute he was and that he was beautiful and shiny. They were the dream team from the get go.

Part Three:
The Newborn Days

Chapter Twenty-One
Our First Night at Home

AFTER my parents had left, the four of us were left staring at Sonny and just consuming him. He made the cutest little grunts, snorts and squeaks and we were all completely obsessed with him. I sat and cradled Sonny whilst Archie and Rory watched me breastfeed. I explained what I was doing and how Sonny was drinking his milk. From then on, each time Sonny would cry, Rory would loudly exclaim, "Quick, Mummy, booby milk!" Archie and Rory loved sitting with me whilst I fed Sonny and would watch him gulp his milk and would inevitably fall around laughing when he let out a giant burp.

After Sonny had had a feed, I left Andrew and the boys to coo over the baby some more whilst I ran myself a bubble bath. I expect it's not recommended so soon after giving birth but aside from my shower post labour, I hadn't had chance to freshen up and I really wanted a quick, hot bubbly soak. It was incredibly satisfying and just what I needed. I got out of the bath, in to some fresh pyjamas and Andrew ordered us all a takeaway for tea.

Andrew and Sonny stayed downstairs, presumably this was when Sonny was introduced to FIFA, and I put Archie and Rory to bed. I gave them the biggest cuddle and the excitement must have exhausted them as they were asleep in minutes.

Andrew brought Sonny and his Moses basket upstairs, and Sonny and I spent the night sleeping, feeding, winding and changing. It was perfect and beautiful.

Andrew had the foresight to bring up a multitude of snacks and drinks (breastfeeding makes you ravenous!) so Sonny and I were both set to pull an all-nighter. I was exhausted, but the very best kind of exhausted. I let Andrew sleep as I knew he'd be on big kid duty the next day and in between feeding, I'd be able to snooze and take it easy. As exhausted as I was, the middle of the night bonding with Sonny was just beautiful. The house was silent and it felt like Sonny and I were the only people awake in the whole world.

Chapter Twenty-Two
The First Few Newborn Days

THE day after Sonny and I got home, a midwife and midwifery student came to see how we were. This is my third time, you'd think I'd have remembered by now, but alas I was braless, hair dishevelled and in bed when they called. It's all a bit of a whirlwind, isn't it?!

The two midwives were lovely and happily came upstairs to see us both (my sciatica was still rife, so I was grateful for not having to move) and the only difference between seeing them this time around compared to my other two children, was their PPE. You sort of get used to it in the end, all the masks and visors. A few days later we had to go in to hospital for Sonny's heal prick test (I've no idea if this was because of Covid or the hospital's latest policy, but I'm sure they did it at home the previous two times). Taking my newborn in to a germy hospital was the last thing I wanted to do but it was a Sunday and it was really quiet.

A few days after that our lovely health visitor came over, again the only difference was she was dressed head to toe in PPE. Then a few days after that was our final midwife visit. This time we went to the local children's centre. They were short-staffed, running an hour late (none of this was a problem at all, I was and am fully appreciative of how run off their feet they were) but the appointment itself was pretty typical of most of my antenatal and postnatal appointments. Rushed. Actually, my other postnatal appointments had been fine. My antenatal ones had too, really, but they were just so inconsistent and I hadn't seen the same midwife more than once. Again, nobody's fault. It just leaves you feeling a bit deflated.

As soon as I walked in I was told we'd have to be quick as they were running late and the building was going to be closing for the day. Sonny was weighed but it wasn't recorded in his red book (I didn't realise this until afterwards otherwise I'd have mentioned it). I told the midwife I had the baby blues and although I'm sure that's all it was, that I would keep an eye on it, as I hadn't felt this sad or overwhelmed with my other two. I was feeling very sad and very cross all at once and it was confusing, because at the same time I felt the happiest I'd ever felt. It was such an oxymoron. It wasn't nice and I was out of my comfort zone, I didn't know what these emotions or feelings were and it was isolating and confusing. I know for a fact that I put up an act and pretended I was doing better than I was, because I am stubborn and terrible at asking for help, but when she discharged us, I felt a little flat. Not because I didn't want to be discharged, but because I felt tired, overwhelmed, rushed and an inconvenience.

I'd walked to the other side of the village, days after giving birth with some intense physical pain and everything else that comes with just giving birth and I just felt like it was a pointless appointment. Maybe I had made more of it because I hadn't been allowed to see anybody and the reality of how my fourth trimester was going to look like was a bit overwhelming, I don't know. Writing it down and thinking about it properly, it wasn't the midwives' fault at all. She was rushed and stressed and I know what I'm like. I will have gone in all jolly, smiley and chatty and I will have massively downplayed my cry for help. I have no doubt in my mind that if I'd have asked her for help or told her I was struggling with my emotions and not ready to be discharged then she would have made another appointment for me. She's not a mind reader.

It's just hard sometimes, isn't it? Especially when you're a stubborn ass.

Chapter Twenty-Three
Loneliness

BEING a parent in normal circumstances can be incredibly lonely. In my personal opinion, it is the most joyous and wonderful thing I have ever done and ever will do, but it can still be incredibly isolating. The reason (some) parents enjoy baby classes and soft play so much is because there are actual other adult humans to speak to. That, and it helps you build a routine in to your week.

Not everybody likes soft play and a routine, but a lot of people do. It's a necessity for some people's mental health. Once Covid hit, parents had to parent without their usual support and routine. If parenting felt isolating before, the pandemic was about to crank it up a notch.

On a personal level, I thrive in a routine and baby groups. I enjoy speaking to other adults, I enjoy a routine and it's a part of the baby and childhood days that I really enjoy. My family don't live close by and a lot of my really good friends don't either. I work from home and my husband works long days. I thrive on seeing my local (and amazing) friends, and going to a baby or toddler group a couple of times a week. When Covid struck, not only did it mean parent's routines were out of kilter, but when it came time to do normal things again, it was hard to do so. I hadn't driven for months. I hadn't seen anybody. I'd not been to any shops and apart from taking the children on walks for our exercise, I hadn't left the house. When my lovely health visitor would come to the house to see Sonny and I, I wouldn't stop talking! I told her anything and everything. It's like I didn't know how to function as a social being any more. The same came to driving and leaving the house. My anxiety had risen exponentially and I was genuinely concerned for my mental health and how going forward my life would look. I wasn't used to driving, I wasn't used to people and all of a sudden, I had become scared of my own shadow. If I was driving, I would panic thinking about what would happen to my children if I crashed. And I mean real panic. I couldn't breathe properly and I would have anxiety attacks just thinking about being in a car.

The same went for people. Particularly in shops. I had been to the occasional shop since the pandemic began, but not many because my husband was the designated shopper. When I went in to a shop, I would imagine everybody had Covid and I would contract it and give it to my children and I just wanted to get in and out as fast as I could. Without a doubt, my mental health was suffering and I feared what my life would look like post- pandemic. I couldn't just switch off my fears and carry on as before. There was a huge block in my mind and I couldn't shift it. I wanted to get out of the house which was slowly resembling a prison, but I was terrified to do so and just wanted to stay home.

When Sonny was first born, I spent most of the first few weeks hibernating and staying in our safe, little cocoon. My husband was on paternity leave so he would do the school runs and as we weren't allowed to see anybody or do anything, I could unapologetically stay in bed with my brand new, little baby. One day, when Sonny was a couple of weeks old, my eldest asked if all of us could pick him up from school. He was so proud of his baby brother and he wanted us all to go and get him.

I was still suffering from severe sciatic pain so I had avoided moving too much up until now, but I decided a nice walk (hobble/shuffle) would be just what we all needed; and I missed picking up my boy from school. He always has the biggest smile on his face when he sees me, I'd missed that. So I got Sonny all wrapped up and tucked him in to his pram. I proudly pushed him the mile to school, with my husband and Rory. It was a lovely, albeit painful, walk.

However, as soon as I got to the school gates, my breathing became heavier. Lovely friends wanted to do what everyone does when somebody has a baby and peek in to the pram for a look. I felt physically sick. The thought of Sonny getting sick made me feel physically ill. I had managed to protect him for nine months and now, in the midst of a global pandemic, he was out in the world and I felt like I couldn't keep him safe. I worried that my friends would think I was rude but all I wanted to do was run home. He was fine, of course, but I got him home and ran us both a bath. I knew my mental health was something I had to keep an eye on and also knew a big part of it was postpartum hormones.

I had never been a germophobe before so this was completely new territory and I didn't like it. The next time I did the school run, when Andrew was back at work, it was raining. Sonny had his rain cover on and I remember feeling so happy. His pram had its own little hazmat suit and my anxiety levels were much lower. He was just so little. A tiny (not so tiny at 10lb+) little newborn and I just wanted to protect him.

Chapter Twenty-Four
Postnatal Support

I will start off by saying, our NHS trust and local children's centre completely went above and beyond to ensure postnatal support was delivered as normally as possible. Things were so different, of course, but if you needed to access a particular service then it was always achievable, just in a different way than usual. I don't know what other trusts offered and if that was consistent across the country, or if it was because I was fortunate enough not to need any further support outside the usual postnatal care, but I certainly found myself supported and looked after and felt that if there were any questions or services I needed to access, then I would have had help with that.

This was my third baby and my third time breastfeeding. I was fortunate enough not to have any problems or pain and breastfeeding support was never a service I needed to access. Pre-Covid days, there was an abundance of breastfeeding support groups, up and down the country, run by both children's centres and which were privately run too. When Covid hit, these support groups had to close and many of them had to become virtual/online sessions instead. Our local children's centre did this.

They could still run, but they had to become virtual sessions. I can't help but worry about those women who did need support and would have struggled without a face to face (or rather face to boob) consultation. Don't get me wrong, our local trust did everything they could to work around the Covid restrictions, but it was still something else the pandemic took away.

When women and babies struggle on their breastfeeding journey, it's usually because of pain, discomfort, undiagnosed allergies, tongue tie or latch issues. All of these issues that would be harder for a first-time mum to know how to deal with or what to look out for.

Irrespective of how great it was that there was still an option to have a support session, it still must have been so much harder to do that online. The breastfeeding peer supporter would need to watch baby feed to be able to offer any help, I imagine if you are trying to feed babe then also pointing your phone or laptop at yourself whilst doing so must have been a challenge. Women with partners could have helped of course, but not all women have support at home so this is just another roadblock created by the fact that services had to halt or at least change because of the current situation.

Of course, health visitors and GPs were still available to diagnose tongue tie or allergies, but a lot of procedures had been delayed if they weren't an emergency, meaning women had to pay to go private, which of course not everybody could afford. Also, often a person specifically trained in breastfeeding would need to be the person to help with breastfeeding concerns, and away from any physical concerns, sometimes women just needed to chat and ask questions and just be in a community of women going through the same. Women wanting to know if pain was normal, what type of pain, how long it should last, what a let-down was, how often to feed, how long they would leak for, if there were items in their diet they should restrict and a million other questions that breastfeeding mothers will inevitably have because their breasts don't come with an instruction manual.

Regardless of how you choose to feed your child, you should have access to support. I can only write about breastfeeding because that is what I know, but I don't doubt for a single second that women who formula fed their babies needed extra support too and that they struggled with services being cut off. It was nobody's fault, everybody did what they could to offer Covid-secure classes, but I know for some it just wasn't enough.

A lot of women (me, absolutely me) find it incredibly hard to ask for help. Whether it's stubbornness, because they feel as though they should be able to handle it or because they don't want to bother anybody. It's common and I probably know more people who struggle to seek help than people who don't. When Covid hit, services were still there but they were harder to access unless you were able to ask for help. Nobody was going to do a weekly welfare check just to ask how you were, and you now couldn't pop along to a breastfeeding café or health visitor clinic. You had to specifically phone and make an appointment and actually ask for help and admit you needed it.

I know of a lot of women at this time (me included) who struggled with something and because it was harder to access support, just ignored it. This ultimately led to further stress and the issue not being resolved. I could barely walk at the end of my pregnancy (sciatica) and I naively presumed it would ease up when the baby came. It did, eventually, and now presents itself as a flare up every now and again, but it didn't ease up as quickly as I'd hoped or imagined. This in turn caused me to panic because I assumed I'd be in agony forever and I started worrying about how I would manage the school run again, go shopping again, play with the boys or when I began working again- if or how I would sit at a sewing machine. I was in a lot of pain and it was hard to imagine life any other way, and I panicked. All I needed to do was phone the doctor and come up with a care plan, but I was reluctant. I was convinced that they wouldn't do anything until I was at least six weeks postpartum because that's when you have a doctor check anyway and when your body should have healed, or at least mainly healed. It was my husband that pushed me to phone the doctor in the end, I was crying every day and shuffling around. Flinching and wincing and just not having a great time of it.

I ended up having a telephone consult and the most understanding doctor. He gave me a prescription for some strong painkillers (he referred to them as the 'big boys') and referred me to physiotherapy. He said if it was still this painful in two months, he would refer me for an MRI to see if it could offer more answers. He reminded me that I'd just grown and laboured a 10lb 2oz human and to be kinder to myself and to give myself time. He said (more than once) that I'd absolutely done the right thing by asking for help and he would do what he could to help me.

He phoned me a couple of weeks later to check on my progress and all together, asking for help when I was struggling was the best decision I made. Without my husband pushing me however, I don't think I'd have phoned. I didn't want to bother anybody. Had Covid not have happened, I would have probably walked (hobbled, shuffled, driven) to the children's centre, where you didn't need to make an appointment, and just mentioned it to one of the health visitors. I would have felt as though I was there anyway, to have Sonny weighed, so I wasn't making as much of a fuss. If a friend would have said this to me, I'd have told her not to be so silly, but it's different when it's yourself isn't it?

I don't know if it's because we're stubborn or British (stiff upper lip) or because we just don't want to make a fuss, but I do know that accessing help when you had to ask for it, was a lot harder and I am sure contributed to raising cases in undiagnosed pain, postnatal depression, women stopping breastfeeding and other issues.

Chapter Twenty-Five
The Newborn Photoshoot

MY maternity photoshoot came as a sort of two for one deal. Bump to baby. This was the shoot that very nearly didn't go ahead and I am so happy it did. Sonny was 8 days old when we had a newborn shoot in our home. Just two weeks later, the prime minister announced lockdown 2.0. I am so very thankful of the timing surrounding birth and the second lockdown. I was already really struggling that I couldn't introduce Sonny to anybody, if the photoshoot had been taken away too, I know I would have really struggled.

Hand sanitiser became everybody's favourite accessory, and after suitably sanitising ourselves, we had a really lovely and very relaxed photoshoot. It felt so incredibly normal and I'm so grateful for that. It was one of the only normal things we were able to do in a less than normal time.

My friend, who was the photographer, would be one of the only people to have met Sonny whilst he was a newborn. It felt very unnatural for me not to hand him to her for a cuddle, we just had to cope with socially distanced cooing. The virus was invisible, some people were asymptomatic. It felt incredibly alien to me to not gush and parade my baby and insist anyone and everyone have a cuddle (proud parent alert) but it was just so utterly terrifying so we had to keep our distance.

I will always be so thankful for the photographs taken and memories made on that day. It gave us all a chance to get dressed up and have the most intimate and candid moments captured. Life as we knew it felt a million miles away but to be allowed to have a professional capture these moments so we could share them with family and friends was a saving grace. I'll cherish the photographs of my newborn squish and the rest of our team forever and hopefully instead of being reminded how hard and lonely a lot of the newborn days were, I will look at shots captured of us all cuddling and me feeding Sonny and be transported back to the most cosiest and perfect little newborn baby bubble. To anybody considering a photographer capturing some newborn candid moments (feeding, burping, cradling etc), in or out of a pandemic, I absolutely recommend it. The newborn phase zooms by way too quickly and having photographs to look back on is just magical.

Chapter Twenty-Six
Lockdown 2.0

THE 31st October 2020 saw the beginning of lockdown 2.0. This time, schools, colleges and universities would stay open, but anything besides those, essential shops and healthcare, would have to immediately close. We were given a four-week end date and told to sit tight and stay home until then. This meant we couldn't have any visitors for Sonny and apart from the school run for my eldest, we would just stay home and have lots of cuddles. This lockdown went by, for me, in a bit of a blur to be honest. I had just about got my head around the no visitors rule so we just had our routine of doing the school run and then adapting to a family of five. If only past me had known that the subject of having visitors for Sonny would become a moot point, I wouldn't have had to worry and fret so much. It was such an odd time. Legally, people couldn't come and visit my newborn baby. How bizarre and sad is that?

My husband was off work for some of lockdown 2.0 on annual leave, so he would do the school runs when he could and Sonny and I had some beautiful 1:1 bonding time. We made the most of being allowed out for walks and it was at a beautiful time of year (autumn — my favourite) so we just embraced it as much as we could. I was still recovering physically and emotionally so we just enjoyed bobbing along. My husband was fantastic; he'd bring me food whilst I cuddled and fed Sonny.

We did a lot of nothing those first few weeks and it was really lovely. It was an incredibly bittersweet time; It was beyond disappointing that we couldn't share and celebrate Sonny with our friends and family, but it was so amazing that we could just bask in our newborn bubble and do nothing but bond with Sonny, cuddle him, spend extra special time with our other two children and just really relish in being a unit and introducing a new member to our team. It was easy to forget the country was in lockdown because we were still in our newborn bubble, making the most of the hibernation days and binge-watching Gilmore Girls. We were told the end date (2nd December) this time so it felt easier, knowing the end was in sight. It was just a short, sharp lockdown to get the infection rate back down and get back in control of the virus. That was the plan anyway. I believe it worked like that initially, but the cases soon rose again.

The 2nd December soon came around and plans for how the country would proceed followed. The nation wanted to know what they were allowed to do and how to plan. The government decided there would be a relaxation in rules over the Christmas period to allow for family get-togethers and then the plan was to return to the tier system afterwards.

A few days later, a beacon of light appeared when the government announced that a support bubble could be formed with families with a baby under 12 months. That meant, regardless of your tier, you could regularly see one chosen household and social distancing didn't need to be adhered to. This news was wonderful and a lifeline to so many. Childcare support bubbles already existed, but these state that the adults can't mix socially with the chosen childcare, you just need to drop the children off.

This new baby support bubble meant people could get the

support and help they needed. It was a huge relief and a great day for isolated new parents. This is where it got a little complicated though, and sadly we weren't really able to make use of the support bubble. We decided to ask my husband's parents to join our bubble. My parents had (for twenty minutes when I came home from the hospital) technically met Sonny, so we thought we'd invite Andrew's parents over for a week. They don't live close so it would never have been a situation where we'd pop over to each other's houses for a cuppa.

At this time, we were in tier three, and his parents tier two. Understandably, they were scared of infection rates, cases and their health so they chose not to come. It was okay, we fully understood, this virus was so new and people were scared. I was scared of our local supermarket at this point so I don't blame them for not wanting to leave home just yet. Next, we asked our parents if they would like to join our bubble. They live closer and could make it for the odd day here and there. They joined our bubble and a couple of days later they were able to join us for the day. It was lovely. They got to meet Sonny properly, play with the other two too and we exchanged Christmas presents.

Royal Mail were swamped at this point so we didn't want to post anything, so we were grateful that we could give my parents presents that I'd bought for my side of the family to door stop deliver for us! Little did we know, this would be the last time we would see them for a while. They had plans to see other members of our family over the allotted Christmas period (the government relaxed social meetings for Christmas), so we decided we'd go to their house in the New Year instead. Sadly, this didn't happen due to a third lockdown and a second bout of shielding for my dad.

Chapter Twenty-Seven
Registering Sonny's Birth

REGISTERING births during the pandemic had taken a back seat. Pre-Covid, one would have six weeks to decide on their baby's name and to formally register them. You could go to the registry office alone or as a family, there were options and you could make the day a special one. When the first lockdown happened, there was a halt on registering births and subsequently, there became a back log for some months later. Each area of the country differed and actually our area didn't suffer too much with delays and I was able to register Sonny within the usual timeframe. However, I had friends up and down the country who were still unable to get an appointment to register their child months and months after they had been born.

We registered Sonny when he was three weeks old. We had the choice of going to the city centre to register him or to walk to our village registry office. We decided on the latter. With our second son, we had done the same and I fondly remember making an afternoon of it. It's an exciting, memorable and significant day. With Rory, myself, my husband and Archie walked in to the village, registered Rory's birth, took some obligatory birth certificate selfies and went for hot chocolate and cake afterwards. With Sonny, we couldn't do this. The shine was taken off his special day but we still managed a nice walk. Well, it was still a shuffle from me, but it was still nice.

Archie was at school so Andrew, Rory, Sonny and I took a walk in to the village. Only one person was allowed in to the registry office and although babes in arms didn't count, they did say if you could help it, not to. As I was the one with the boobs, I waited outside on a bench with Rory and Sonny whilst Andrew registered Sonny's birth. It felt a bit sad really. Naming a child is a big responsibility. He had become official and legal and I wanted to celebrate with cake! Sonny's name was particularly poignant in the current climate. We had always liked the name Sonny. As soon as we heard it, we put it on our list. We loved how it sounded with our other children's names.

As 2020 progressively got worse, we decided to name him Sonny as a reminder of him being the sunshine we all needed in this otherwise shocker of a year. He will always be our baby born in the midst of a global pandemic therefore the happiness amongst the sad. He is pure joy, optimism and hope and that's what we wanted his name to reflect. So it wasn't just a name and a piece of paper. It was an important day, so it was a shame that we couldn't register him together and go out for a drink afterwards but it doesn't take away the importance of Sonny and the reason behind his name.

Chapter Twenty-Eight
Surprising Struggles

HAVING a newborn when the world had essentially stood still, was strange. There were lots of positives hidden amongst the abundance of negatives; but there were also some struggles that had come as a complete surprise to me and that I had not even considered whilst I was pregnant.

Feeding in public. When my other two children were newborns, if they needed feeding, I would stop and feed them, wherever and whenever. If I was in a shopping centre, I'd find a bench or a seat and feed them. If I was walking through the village and it was a bit cold, I'd nip in to a coffee shop and feed them. If I was in a bank, I'd sit and feed them. If I was in a restaurant, I'd carry on eating one handed and feed my baby. There was never anywhere I felt uncomfortable or unable to feed. I never even considered that during lockdown when everything was closed, it would be incredibly hard to just stop and feed your baby. Coffee shops were no longer open for you to nip in to. Everything was 'click and collect'. You couldn't access anywhere to have a quick sit and feed.

When Sonny was brand new, I had gone in to town for a few postpartum jumpers and jeggings. We weren't in lockdown at this point so shops were open, but there were still a lot of restrictions and one-way systems.

Some seating had been cordoned off and they basically

wanted you in, to shop and to get out again. Out of nowhere, like they do, Sonny began whaling. He was inconsolable and I knew the only thing that would soothe him would be milk. Do you know where I ended up feeding him? A photo booth. No joke. There was nowhere else. It was throwing it down with rain outside, the indoor seating had been cordoned off and it was all one way so if I had walked any further to find seating, it would have taken ages and try telling a tiny baby to wait five minutes. I had to get creative. I parked the pram, pulled open the little, orange curtain and perched on the stool. I had to tuck my elbows right in as it was a bit of a squeeze, but I managed to make it work.

Another time I had just left the pharmacy to walk home and the milk scream began. I was too far from home but we were in lockdown so nowhere besides the essentials were open. It was freezing cold so I was reluctant to feed him outside, he was still so new. So I turned back with the view of nipping back inside the pharmacy and feeding him in there. Ordinarily, I wouldn't have asked. The Equality Act 2010 protects all breastfeeding mothers meaning nobody can say no or ask you to move.

Pre- Covid I'd have just found a chair, or asked for one, and fed my baby. Now though, it was different. As I turned back to go in to the pharmacy, I saw the sign stating only one person to be allowed in at a time, and there was a small queue of people waiting their turn. I didn't know what to do, my baby needed feeding. I wasn't a customer. I didn't want to feed him outside nor did I want to join the queue and wait. He was screaming. I ended up poking my head through the door and telling the pharmacist that I knew about the rule but that the baby needed feeding and asked if I could possibly sit in the corner (out the way of any other customers or staff) to feed him. She didn't hesitate in letting me in and I assume by the volume my child was reaching that no customers in the queue were cross that I was allowed to go in. Sorry not sorry if they were.

Then there's the mask. In all the commotion to make the baby stop crying, I had completely forgotten to put on my face mask. It was only half way through his feed that I realised and reached in to my pocket to grab my mask and put it on. I was already hot and flustered at this point and now I felt as though I was suffocating. Just an occurrence I hadn't really considered about worrying about when I was pregnant.

Now there were restrictions everywhere we went, it made it really difficult to feed Sonny wherever he needed. I would make sure I offered him a feed just before I left the house and just had to hope the pram would send him to sleep. I'd make sure I would have blankets with me in case I had to feed him outside on a bench so I could just bundle him up and keep him toasty. School runs were stressful because of having to leave at a particular time. I couldn't just wait until his next feed and then set off. Not that feeding on the school run would have been particularly easy to do before Covid life but it would have been easier because there would have been more options available to stop and top him up.

Baby changing. If I left the house, which wasn't often these days, I would prepare to not be too long, as changing Sonny's nappy would become difficult. Akin to feeding, there were limited places I could just nip in to, to change his nappy. Coffee shops were closed, restaurants and pubs too. With my other sons, if they needed a nappy change whilst out, I would nip in to a coffee shop or restaurant, use their facilities and usually buy a polite drink to take away with me. This just wasn't possible any more. Even the fast-food chains were 'drive-thru' only. Even if I did venture further afield, to a shopping centre or supermarket where they had baby changing rooms, the virus had made me so paranoid and so aware of potential germs that the last thing I wanted to do was lay down my newborn on a dirty surface. No amount of cleaning or antibacterial wiping down would have put me at ease, so I just avoided going out too much as changing him, or not being able to, had just become too stressful.

Chapter Twenty-Nine
Keeping in Touch

THANK goodness for video calls, social media and all manner of modern technology to assist communication. Our little baby was growing at a rapid rate and we were the only people who could witness it. I will always be thankful (maybe not the right word but you know what I mean) that we went through all of this in a time where technology connected us all. Sonny would only know his grandparents through a screen at this point but it was better than nothing. He could hear and interact with them and if that's all we could get right now, then so be it. It wouldn't compare to a kiss or a cuddle but those days would come. Photo messages, social media and video calls. It was all instantaneous and I will always be grateful for that.

Ironically, life was busier than ever right now. The world had stood still but taking care of a newborn, entertaining a pre-schooler and home-schooling an almost-seven-year-old in between various school closures was full on. I was exhausted (I had a newborn that didn't sleep and I don't drink coffee) and busy, and that is why I am so grateful for how instant communication was these days. Don't get me wrong, I would have loved nothing more than to phone my parents regularly or write to family members, but I had next to nothing left and I just couldn't. Video calls, text messages and a social media post was the perfect vehicle to enable family members to see how Sonny (and we) were doing but that didn't take time away from home-schooling or anything else.

I would upload daily photos to social media on an account that could only be seen by family. I have done this since my eldest was born as a keepsake for him but also for family members to see what he had been up to. This way, if they wanted to, they could check in and see how the kids were growing and what they'd been up to and then, when we could, we would video call grandparents so they could check in.

People will always have an opinion about social media. It may be favourable or it may not. But whatever your opinion, and however you use it, no one can deny the incredible way it can be used to bring together friends and family. Social restrictions lasted a long time which meant family and friends went a long time without seeing each other.

The technology available also made for an excellent time to have to home-school. The independent tasks were set via an app on my phone, which we would tackle around feeding Sonny and playing with Rory, and the live classrooms were done over video calling on the laptop, and after the first week of getting used to it, Archie could access this by himself. It worked very well and again, I'm so grateful that if we had to go through all this then it was at a time of social media, technology and instant communication. Everything we needed was at a scroll, a swipe or a click of a button and I'm incredibly thankful for that.

Chapter Thirty
A Vaccine

YES! At last! What we had all (most) been waiting for. Our incredible scientists had been working around the clock to find a vaccine against Covid-19. Amongst all of the devastation could now be triumph. This was momentous and a huge cause for celebration. Before Christmas there would be talk of it becoming available soon, but I don't think anybody really believed it. There were cynics, of course, saying it had been rushed and it wasn't safe. But it hadn't been rushed. The base vaccine already existed, it just needed developing for this particular strain. Amongst the cynics, most people were elated and overjoyed that it now meant there was an end in sight.

Quickly after the vaccine had been brought to light, it was suggested that breastfeeding mothers, pregnant women and women hoping to become pregnant in the next few months should not have the vaccine. As a breastfeeding mother, I was heartbroken. I didn't want to stop feeding my baby to get the vaccine but I didn't want to not get the vaccine and put myself and others at risk. It wasn't something I would have to think about any time soon as I knew I'd be low on the priority list to receive it and thankfully before I could worry about it any longer, the advice for breastfeeding mother's changed and it was then suggested that it was absolutely fine to have the vaccine whilst breastfeeding. Phew. At the time of writing, I haven't been invited for my vaccine just yet but as soon as I am, I will get it. I believe if you are pregnant then the vaccine should be discussed with your GP and the benefits of it should highly outweigh the negatives, but women trying for a baby now don't need to avoid the vaccine like previously suggested.

On the 8th December 2020, a ninety-year-old woman from the UK (Margaret Keenan) became the first person in the world to receive the Pfizer Covid-19 vaccine. This felt like the beginning of the end. We knew we had a long way to go before life resembled any sort of normality but this was a turning point and something I and so many others were celebrating. The vaccine started being rolled out very quickly. It was an exciting time. My husband got his shortly after and we knew it would only be a matter of time before life started looking like it did before. Our parents would be getting their vaccine soon too, and things were looking up. This is what we had been waiting for. The vulnerable were now being protected and the fog was lifting.

Mid-February, the prime minister would announce that there was end in sight and he gave dates of when he expected social restrictions to ease and eventually lift.

This was all because of the vaccine. It was working magnificently and millions of people had already had their first vaccination. The nation had gone a whole year of being told to avoid people, only to leave the house if absolutely necessary and to avoid all physical contact.

There was the obvious and expected elation of being given a potential (it wasn't set in stone just yet) date of getting back to normal, but also the less expected but not all together surprising anxiety and utter fear about being allowed to go back to our everyday lives. We were still living in a pandemic, we still had to wear masks and still had to avoid everybody. We had become accustomed to this new way of life because we were told it was safe and it would protect us and our families. My little baby had barely met anybody, all because it was the right thing to do. Although a huge part of me wanted to rejoice and couldn't wait to do all of the things with him that I'd dreamed and to introduce him to family and friends, there was a huge part of me that was utterly terrified.

Chapter Thirty-One
Jabs — Baby Ones, Not Covid.

WHEN Sonny was eight weeks-old, he was called up for his routine vaccinations. The day in itself wasn't particularly different to how it had been with my other two children, except you had to go alone and wear a mask. I would have gone alone anyway so today really was no different to how it would have been pre-Covid. The only difference was the germs and my paranoia and a feeling I hadn't had before.

As I sat in the doctor's surgery, I was acutely aware of sick people. The surgery had got rid of most of the seats so you were really spaced out from one another, and the majority of appointments were currently taking place over the phone, but it didn't stop this hormonal and panicky mum to a very tiny human worrying incessantly over any and all potential germs.

I think there was only one other person in the waiting room, and they had a baby with them so it was likely that they were there for the same reason I was. But I couldn't help it. I was willing Sonny to stay asleep so he could stay tucked up safe in his pram. I didn't want him to wake, because then he would probably cry and then I'd have to get him out and feed him and he'd be exposed to the germs of the waiting room.

Every now and again the realisation that my mental health wasn't so great and my paranoia was a little too prominent became clear. I could see it, I could feel it, but I couldn't help it. I just wanted to protect my little baby.

His jabs went fine, he let out a little squeak but I immediately fed him which soothed him instantly. He went back to sleep, I bundled him up and we got out of the doctors' surgery. The nurse had reminded me that his meningitis jab might make him sleepy and oh it did! We had a lovely, lazy day after that filled with snuggly, sleepy cuddles.

Chapter Thirty-Two
A Pandemic Christmas

CHRISTMAS 2020 was a good one. Of course, the state of the world was terrifying but being forced to stay at home actually made for a pretty perfect Christmas Day. It's not that we didn't miss our extended family, because we did, but we didn't have to rush to be anywhere or worry about which of the children's presents to bring with us. I love a loud and busy Christmas Day but I also loved this quiet and calm one, particularly with a brand-new baby. I didn't want to be rushing around right now and being forced to have a quiet one was great.

My husband was supposed to be working Christmas day. That would have made the day considerably less fun, but amazingly somebody swapped shifts with him so he was able to be home all day. We ate delicious food, watched the kids open and play with their presents, took thousands of photos of the boys in their cute Christmas clothes and Facetimed both sides of the family. We played games, ate, played some more and of course ate some more too. It really was a great day.

I was so worried about this month. December is always a month of cramming as much Christmas inspired activities in as possible. There are always nativities, Christingles, Christmas Fayres and of course, Santa's grotto. I was so sad that the pandemic would put a stop to so many fun things. It did stop them, but not completely. Through the creativity of individuals and organisations, December 2020 still managed to be really fun and certainly memorable.

Santa's grottos were banned, but the big guy himself had a word with the elves and they decided to create a drive thru grotto. The idea was that you stay in your car but with the windows down, you slowly drive through an interactive experience, chatting to cheeky elves on the way through, ending your visit by driving up to Mr. and Mrs. Claus. He had a present waiting for all of the children and their faces just lit up. It was truly magical. Magical, that is, when your newborn isn't screaming his little socks off, but let's focus on the cute happy bit of this memory. Besides, we pulled up behind Santa's workshop and gave Sonny a feed and he was all good after that and the other two had a chance to open and play with their gifts from Father Christmas.

Christingle still went ahead, just in the form of printed colouring sheets for the children and a DIY Christingle. Our neighbour (and friend) dropped off the kit for the boys so we were still able to take part in this Christmas tradition. All was not lost.

The local community had organised a Christmas lights competition around the village. It was wonderful to see the effort of so many and how beautiful the village shone in all its twinkly lights. Each weekend we would wrap up warm and cosy and take a different route through the village, looking at all of the beautiful lights.

Father Christmas also did a drive by in a neighbouring village. It was throwing it down with rain, freezing cold, but it was one of the most glorious sights seeing my two big kids enamoured with Father Christmas. I put Sonny in the Tula, so he was snug and warm and slept throughout the excitement, and we watched and waited for the sleigh to ride past. It was wonderful.

I really needn't have worried about Christmas and the festivities being ruined for the children by the pandemic. So much was cancelled and couldn't go ahead, but so much took its place and I am so thankful that Sonny's first Christmas was still so magical and that my other two boys had a spectacular time too.

Chapter Thirty-Three
Goodbye 2020 — Don't Let the Door Slam You on the Way Out!

ASIDE from the obvious, becoming a mum to my third son, 2020 had been a shocker. It was the year the world stood still. Covid had consumed the entire globe and it is a year no one will forget. Early on in the pandemic, people would wish away 2020, I think probably assuming it would all be over by Christmas and that we could start afresh in 2021. This was clearly not the case and so the idea of a usual midnight celebration to bid farewell to the current year and to see in the new with hope and optimism, was fraught. We don't usually celebrate New Year's Eve particularly elaborately, and clearly, this year we couldn't if we wanted to, so we just enjoyed some newborn snuggles, a glass of fizz and left-over Christmas camembert and brie. I wouldn't have wanted it any other way.

Of course nothing would really change, the clock would strike twelve and after midnight it would just be a new day. But now it was 2021, and we all hoped the pandemic would be confined to one year and we could move on, it just felt like this was the new normal now. We'd had almost twelve months of it and each time we dared to dream a way out of it, we'd end up in another lockdown or a new variant of the virus would be discovered or death rates would rise. Inarguably, the best scientists in the world had done an incredible job of creating a vaccine, and in no time at all really, but still; the start of 2021 and seeing us still facing this as our new life, it just felt a bit anticlimactic.

Nobody seemed forward in wishing one another a 'Happy New Year'. Of course, optimism was on the horizon but this new way of life wasn't one we wanted to get used to nor continue for much longer. We wanted to get on with the rest of our lives. It was so unfair on the children. Childhoods go by in the blink of an eye, you never want to miss a moment, and the very fact that they'd been robbed of an entire year of memories just seemed cruel. I just hope they look back on it and see more positives than negatives. The hanging out with their brothers every day, not needing to rush around, doing school at home. I don't want them worrying about what they missed but instead, what they gained. Family memories and slow weekends.

Chapter Thirty-Four
Lockdown 3.0

BOXING Day came, tiers were added (we remained in tier three, lots of the country moved to tier four), New Year's eve was celebrated with cheese and prosecco, and on 4th January, lockdown 3.0 was announced. All non-essential travel was banned and although technically (I think) we could have travelled to see our support bubble, we decided it wasn't safe so went back to how we were before. My dad was told to shield because of his health, being on the roads (particularly at this time of year) wasn't the best idea, so we sadly decided to go back to life before the bubble.

There was a vaccine and better weather in our future so we knew soon we'd be able to have outdoor meets so we just hung tight. So although we weren't able to fully make use of the support bubble, I am so pleased for those new parents that could. It's what they needed after being isolated throughout the pandemic and to have somebody hold the baby whilst you go for a pee or have a drink is just bliss and something not to be taken for granted. I'm so happy for those that needed it and were able to fully benefit from their baby support bubble.

Over the Christmas period, the government had relaxed some rules about socialising. Although I don't blame anyone for seeing people over Christmas, it was inevitable that cases and deaths would be on the rise as a result of this. Sadly, this is exactly what happened and the day before the majority of children were due back at school, the prime minister announced (at eight p.m., nothing like giving notice huh?) that there was going to be a third national lockdown, including keeping children (except the children of key workers) off of school. So, alongside most other parents in the country, I embarked on my second stint of home-schooling. The first time this happened, I had one less child and my eldest (the home-schoolee) was in the year below, thus the workload less. I had to prepare myself for teaching my six-year-old, entertaining my three-year-old and being a 24/7 milk bar for my newborn. I added prosecco to the shopping list that night. And chocolate. Lots of chocolate. Whilst there are no ideal age gaps between your children, I always loved my three-year gaps for so many reasons. Until home-schooling.

Having three children at very different stages of life going through this was hard. My eldest had actual work to learn and knowledge to be absorbed whilst my middle was too young to be able to entertain himself but too old to be content with sitting or lying still whilst Mummy became teacher. Then there was my youngest. He was either feeding, screaming or sleeping. It was a hard act to juggle. I enjoyed so much of it and I was so happy to be able to spend so much time with my sons; but it was hard. I never felt enough. Enough of a teacher, enough of a mother. I tried my best, we all tried our best. And there was certainly no age better than another to have to go through this but I did often think if they were that little bit older it would have been easier. Of course there would be other struggles like more than one of them needing to home-school, I'm not disputing that. Just for me, living through lockdown with a six-year-old, a three-year-old and a newborn, was full on.

We managed to get in to a good rhythm with home-schooling and although my three-year-old was watching way too much *Paw Patrol*, he was happy. The days were hard though. Newborns cry, don't they?

Unless Sonny was being fed or rocked, there were times he just wasn't happy. I couldn't just feed Sonny and put him down, because he didn't want to be put down. So helping Archie with his home learning (and in turn learning myself. Array, split diagraph, fronted adverbial anyone?!) was hard. Some days it was really hard. The perpetual routine of feed, rock, teach, play amongst all three children was a lot to fit in to one day. My poor three-year-old barely got a look in at times. Some days were hard, some days were easier.

When we could, we'd get wrapped up (it was January) and go on a walk. Our walks were becoming samey (lockdown meant you couldn't leave your village or town) but it didn't matter. The fresh air worked wonders. We are lucky enough to live a few minutes from a huge field and park, and the days it had been raining they'd put on their wellies and jump in muddy puddles. Most importantly, on these walks, Sonny would nap! When we got home, I used to will him to stay asleep in his pram (which he mainly did for about twenty minutes) so I could grab some food for the big two and get started with another home-schooling task.

The item I found most used this lockdown was my baby sling. I don't think I could have managed without it!

Sonny didn't always want to go in it (unless I was pacing and jiggling) but when he did, I had my hands again! It was wonderful. It meant I could walk and jiggle Sonny to sleep, teach Archie and simultaneously play with Rory, all whilst getting them their fourteenth snack of the day! It was a very useful item indeed!

The main impact lockdown 3.0 had on my life as a mum with a newborn, were the classes we couldn't go to. I sobbed when we were told these couldn't go forward. I was craving adult company, to do something normal. I had daydreamed, planned and looked forward to a weekly baby massage class and a weekly music class. I looked forward to picking Sonny's favourite outfit, packing a changing bag, driving to the class with him and getting to show him off. I looked forward to having some 1:1 time with Sonny, to chatting to other mums, to seeing old friends and making new ones. I needed these classes. I needed some normal. The classes could not have been more 'Covid secure' but they had to stop over lockdown and it sucked. It really sucked.

The music classes went ahead online and it was lovely that this could happen, and my big two enjoyed helping and joining in, but I was so sad that it couldn't be in person. I couldn't make every class because often home-schooling live online sessions would clash, or Sonny would be napping or Rory would need me, but it was lovely to join in when we could. Stressful (Rory would often just switch the laptop off mid class), but lovely.

Life in lockdown with a newborn had pros and cons. Pros included no early morning school runs with three of them, not worrying about living in my leggings for a little while longer and getting to snuggle my gorgeous, new baby almost all day every day. I kept holding on to these pros when the cons seemed all consuming. The cons list included Sonny not knowing or being able to meet family or friends, him (or I) not being able to attended any baby classes and the biggest thing that I took for granted with my other two was just walking proudly down the street, pushing my pram and having a mosey around a garden centre (these were technically still open but the message was clear, only leave the house if you have to. I don't think a mosey counted as essential) or meeting up with a friend in a coffee shop to eat cake and have a natter whilst the baby snoozed in his pram next to me.

Such simple everyday tasks, but it's what I missed the most. January should have been the time where my eldest would be at school, my middle was going to start preschool and for two and a half days a week it would be just Sonny and I. We should have had a class or two and the time at home would have been spent just cuddling and playing. Instead, I spent a lot of time feeding Sonny and just willing him to not cry whilst I put him down, ran to the kitchen to help my big boy with his school work and then back in to the living room to help my middle boy and then when hearing Sonny cry I'd mutter under my breath and the loop would continue.

It's not that we didn't have fun days and that I didn't love having my boys with me where they were safe and loved and got to play (and fight) with each other every day, but the days were filled with a lot of stress too and it's just not how I (or anyone) had imagined or hoped for.

Chapter Thirty-Five
Summer vs. Winter Lockdowns

THERE were a lot of similarities and a lot of differences between the lockdowns. What made a huge difference, was the weather. The first lockdown, where I was pregnant, felt so much more different to the third lockdown. The sun was shining, we were in the garden most days and had the paddling pool out for the really hot days. There was a socially distanced street party (for VE day), we could leave the house for our hour of exercise without donning a thousand layers of clothing and it just seemed easier somehow. There was an element of novelty for the first lockdown too. It was by no means exciting but it was new and I feel like people were taking it a lot more seriously. Nobody expected it to go on for as long as it did and comparatively to lockdown 3.0 it just seemed easier. Once the first lockdown had relaxed, we were able to go to beaches, to go strawberry picking and have socially distanced picnics. Apart from needing to keep your distance, so many activities were outdoors that it was easy to forget you were living through a global pandemic.

Lockdown 3.0 was in the winter. People were cold, they were fed up, they were struggling financially and it was clear to see that fewer people were taking it seriously. It had almost been a year since the first lockdown and people just wanted their lives back. They wanted to choose whether or not to be sociable. They didn't want to be a prisoner in their own home and they didn't want to go to work each day, terrified of contracting Covid.

The rules and laws surrounding lockdown, tiers and how the public should act were forever changing and not always clear. In the first (summer) lockdown, you could travel to do your exercise, as long as the time it took traveling was less than the time spent there. Lockdown 3.0 (winter) however, the Government website made it clear that you could not travel outside your village/town/part of the city you lived in to exercise. This made lockdown 3.0 a whole lot harder. I love the village I live in but there were only so many times I could enthusiastically suggest a fun walk around the park. It started being more of a chore than anything else. The walls were closing in at this point.

Chapter Thirty-Six
But At Least He Won't Remember

I would often hear, when I uttered how sad I felt about bringing a newborn in to lockdown life, "Don't worry, he won't remember." This was always from well-meaning and caring friends and family, but it didn't help. That was never a doubt in my mind, of course he wouldn't remember. All he wanted and needed were boobs, his parents and his doting big brothers pulling silly faces at him. Sonny remembering was never my problem, it was that I would remember. I would remember that nobody would see him grow. That nobody could meet him, or shower him in kisses and cuddles. I would remember that I couldn't show him off. That I couldn't share those newborn days where although I was exhausted and sore, I was also pumped full of adrenaline, pride and excitement and wanted to share that with people. I will remember that his grandparents, aunties and uncles didn't get to be there from the start. We don't live local to our family so we're used to not seeing them regularly or spontaneously or being able to pop over for a cuppa, but they should have been there from the start. I will remember that he didn't get baptised at 4 months like his brothers and wear the gown I had made from my wedding dress and have a party for him where friends and family could cuddle and relish in him.

I started a 'photo a day' account for my eldest and had

them printed into photobooks until he was four years old. A photo a day of his first four years. I did the same for my second son and the same for Sonny. I will remember the photos I took for all of them and the distinct lack of any other people in Sonny's photos.

I know he won't remember. He won't notice. It will be no different to him. But it will for me. He won't remember the pang of sadness I felt each time I uploaded a photo of him and somebody responded with 'look how big he's getting'. Of course he was getting bigger, and his rolls were a testament to how well he was feeding and that in itself was a compliment to me, but at the time I didn't feel that way. I felt sadness that I couldn't pause time whilst the pandemic went away and let all my friends and family get to know my new, gorgeous and wonderful son. He wouldn't remember, but I would.

Chapter Thirty-Seven
The Health Visitor

OUR health visiting team were fantastic, and we were lucky enough that they were still running weigh in clinics during lockdown. When you are pregnant, you're assigned a health visitor. It is completely optional whether you continue to have visits and appointments but my own experience with the three of my children is nothing short of excellent. I have had a different health visitor for each child and they have all been supportive, kind and available. I find the health visiting team an invaluable service and I feel so lucky to have them.

With my other two sons, the whole health visiting and weighing clinic experience was taken for granted.

Generally, the baby is weighed at birth by the midwife and then again by the midwife at the heal prick test and any subsequent appointments but then once baby has reached a weight the midwives are happy with, you are discharged and handed over to the health visiting team. Your health visitor will usually visit you when the baby is around a week old, and then you're invited to the weigh in clinic as often as you'd like. These usually run weekly and not only are they a chance to have your baby weighed, but if you have any concerns, you can raise them with the health visitor. I used to go fairly often with my second son as he has multiple allergies, they weren't diagnosed until months later so when I was battling with his symptoms, the health visitors were always on hand to give advice and signpost me to further help.

There's not a lot you want more as a mother than to see your little baby gain rolls and put on the pounds. Whether breast or bottle feeding, you want to know the milk is doing its job and they're growing and developing well. Of course wet nappies and tighter clothes are an indication of weight gain, but for some, having the baby weighed and checked weekly or monthly is a safety net and something to look forward to. My husband and I used to put bets on each of our children's next weight, it was a fun game and we used to love seeing who had won to the nearest ounce.

When Covid hit, things had to change. Our local children's centre stayed open but for essential appointments only. Thankfully, this included weigh-in clinics. It wasn't a walk in service now though, you had to make an appointment and stick to your slot. One thing I found so hard throughout the entire pandemic, was not being too early or too late to anything. Especially with children! Everyone who knows me knows I am prompt to everything. I'd rather be an hour early than a minute late. I blame my dad, he's the same. If I'm ever late, it's because of my husband who's the complete opposite.

But with the pandemic, you couldn't be early, nor could you be late. School runs, appointments, anything where you had to stick to an allotted time. There wasn't a lot going on in lockdown but the appointments that were running you had to be specific to when you turned up. I wanted to get Sonny weighed, I wanted to make use of the weigh in clinics but the thought of dragging three children across the village, impossibly timing a newborn's feeds so he didn't cry en route and not being early or late was enough to put me off going altogether.

Before, when you had the luxury of turning up when you could and waiting your turn, it took away all the stress of having to be ready for a certain time. Also, there was home-schooling to consider. My eldest son's school routine was full on at this point. He had Google Live lessons throughout the day interspersed with daily tasks. It was a real juggle and getting us all out to the weigh in clinic just wasn't going to happen.

This is where my wonderful health visitor (Karen) came in. I phoned the main line and asked for a call back, and once I'd heard back, I told her there was nothing I was specifically worried about but I would really like to get Sonny weighed to make sure he's gaining weight as he should, but I was feeling anxious about taking all three kids out. She told me not to worry and she would come to me instead. I didn't even know that was an option but I was so grateful, it took a huge amount of stress away.

Karen came over a few days later armed with her scales and ended up weighing him and measuring his height whilst she was at it, too. She filled out his red book, plotted his growth and reassured me he was following his line perfectly. Whilst she was over, I was able to talk to her about my other children, too. I didn't have any major concerns but I had a couple of things I wanted to air and she was the perfect sounding board. She came in amongst a messy and chaotic home-schooling day, where the big two invariably started showing off, and she didn't bat an eyelid. She then gave me her work mobile number and said I could use it if I had any worries or concerns. I was so happy we'd been assigned Karen. She definitely made things easier and I will always be grateful for that.

Chapter Thirty-Eight
A Fake Christening

CHURCH ceremonies (apart from funerals) had been cancelled. Even though funerals could go ahead, they were still limited in numbers. We wanted to get Sonny christened like his brothers, but it just wasn't an option right now. When I was pregnant with my first son, I remember looking at my wedding dress which was hung on the back of what was about to be our nursery door, and was trying to think of what to do with it. I didn't want to just put it in the attic. It was too special for that and I wanted it to be used again.

I decided to have it made into a christening gown for my children to wear. I decided even if I'd have had a daughter, she may not like or want to wear my wedding dress so there seemed little point in saving it for 'just in case'. I found a company online and sent away my dress. It came back shortly after in the form of a tiny, beautiful and intricate christening gown. I was so happy with my decision and loved the new piece that had been created.

When Archie was four months-old, we had him christened in my family church and the same church my husband and I were married in. We just invited family and my son's godparents and it was a really lovely celebration of Archie's new life.

When Rory was four months-old, we had him christened

too. He also wore the christening gown I'd had made and yet again, we had a small gathering to celebrate our son. This time it was in our local church.

When I was pregnant with Sonny, I knew I wanted to have him christened in the same gown so he'd have to be roughly the same age to have been able to have fitted. As the pregnancy went on, I had just assumed that by the time the baby was around four months-old, either the pandemic would be over or restrictions would have at least been eased. I hadn't counted on things being even worse and christenings not being an option.

I phoned my church and asked the reverend if she would be allowed to perform a socially distanced blessing, rather than a full-blown christening. Just something for the five of us. Sadly, she said she wasn't allowed and we'd have to wait until restrictions eased. We had a positive and uplifting chat about how optimistic we felt and we were sure it wouldn't be long.

Christmas came and went and my optimism was dwindling, so we decided to get creative. Sonny wouldn't be able to get Christened, but there was nothing stopping us getting him dressed in his special gown, the five of us taking a walk down to the church for a bunch of photographs outside it and then coming home for a party and celebration of Sonny. So that's exactly what we did.

I dressed him in the christening gown, put on some white socks and beautiful, fluffy booties and popped him in his pram. We took a slow walk down to church and we got him out for a quick (it was cold!) photoshoot, much to the amusement of passers-by, and then we wrapped him up again and came home to cake, party food, prosecco and games. The party was for the big two really but it was so special to mark the day and to celebrate Sonny. It wasn't a real christening of course but he got to wear the christening gown and we got to eat cake! We will get him christened at some point, when it's legal and it's safe, but I'm so glad we did what we did and made memories and took photographs of him in the christening gown.

Chapter Thirty-Nine
Finally, Baby Classes!

AT the beginning of February 2021, I got a phone call from our local Children's Centre. It was to offer us (Sonny and I) a place on their baby massage class. It wasn't a virtual class, it was to be a face-to-face actual class. To begin at the end of February. The reason this class was allowed to go ahead when nothing else was, was because it was considered to be a 'parental support' group and oh how we needed this parental support. I was completely surprised by my reaction and I just sobbed.

Ugly, couldn't catch my breath style, crying. I presumed I would have to say no because I had my other two at home and home-schooling to do, but she said she had space for us on a Monday, which happens to be my husband's day off. It was perfect. I said yes, of course, and apologised for my startling reaction. The lady on the phone just said it showed what an affect lockdown was having on us (all — but in this case, new mums) and not to apologise.

She then said, "...Now you can have a Mummy and Sonny day." and I sobbed some more. That was exactly it. I was able to reclaim some of the newborn 'normal' time back. I'd be able to pack him a changing bag, put him in the pram and walk him to the other side of the village and have an hour dedicated to us. I would be able to meet new mums (the prospect of speaking to another adult besides my husband was thrilling.)

I know I'm not alone in this and I know this wasn't just a parent thing, I think we were all feeling this! When the phone call was over, I cried some more, text my husband and mum and was completely and utterly grateful that this class could go forward. The main aspects of having a newborn that I was struggling with were not being able to show off my new baby to anybody, not being able to leave the house, Sonny not being able to meet family or friends and I really missed just being able to take a walk in to the village to meet a friend and sit and have cake and a hot chocolate. These short months were going by so quickly and I felt robbed that my pregnancy and newborn days were being spent hidden; so the fact I could now do a normal thing, was completely overwhelming and exciting to me.

Later that month, I would do that baby massage class and it would be wonderful. Sitting in a small group, hugely spaced apart, all wearing masks and no contact allowed was definitely surreal. Bent over my baby, making animated faces to make him smile, and him looking up at me confused because he could only see my eyes, was really sad. But being able to snatch a bit of normality back from the monster that had consumed our lives for the last year, was magnificent.

Chapter Forty
Pandemic Worries and Concerns

BABIES and children are resilient. They make up for lost time very quickly, they learn new skills faster than we could ever imagine and they are just incredibly adaptable. However, it doesn't stop us worrying does it?

My baby hadn't been held by anybody besides the four of us, and my parents twice. He hadn't met anybody else. He hadn't been cooed at or taken part in baby talk or been tickled or sang to, by anybody else. He hadn't had a story read to him by anybody but us. He hadn't seen or met anybody. Sonny didn't care, because he didn't know. He was enamoured with his brothers (and Mummy and Daddy) and that's all he needed. But one day soon, when he would begin to be more alert and more aware, how would he handle meeting and being held by others? Would his experiences hinder his social skills? Would it make him nervous? Honestly, I don't think so. It's not a huge worry. He's a baby and he will change and adapt, but it's still there and it's still a bit of a worry if I think about it too much.

I had seen him at baby massage. I had seen him crane his neck as much as possible to people-watch other babies and parents and to smile at them. I was sure he would adapt just fine, but I didn't know. He was changing so much each day and I didn't know the next time somebody would be able to hold or talk or play with him. I had to trust his smiley and sociable personality that he would be just fine.

I am sure all babies hate car seats. I know all of mine have done at some point. I have memories of singing all manner of nursery rhymes at the top of my lungs until I was able to pull over to feed them, but I don't remember my other two hating the car seat quite as much as Sonny does. Sonny has barely been in the car, quite simply because we are being encouraged to stay at home as much as possible. We go on walks for our exercise and my husband has the car for work and is the designated food shopper, so the children and I walk almost all of the time, Sonny has barely been in the car. The times he has been in the car, if I needed to do an odd shop or if we had an appointment, then he would just scream from the moment he was strapped in until I released him again.

Sonny is an incredibly smiley and happy little man but when he got in the car seat, he was just miserable. He just wasn't used to it. He wasn't used to being squished in to a seat and not being able to see anybody and he just wasn't a fan. My eldest son made up a song for him (It's a Sonny Day for an Elephant to Play) which miraculously worked each time he sang it to him, but only for a couple of run-throughs. So our car journeys would start with a scream then a couple of run-throughs of his favourite song, then the screaming would continue. It was awful. The idea of going in a car with him was anxiety inducing. I knew he'd hate it and I didn't want to put him through that. It was loud too.

Driving with a screaming baby is just horrible. I know as he gets older, he will adapt but right now, whilst he's tiny and doesn't understand, it's just not fun.

Babies respond and react to body language and over the top facial expressions. Sonny loves nothing more than me opening my mouth wide and pulling a goofy face, or pretending to sneeze, or pull kissy faces at him. Thanks to Covid, and the need to wear face masks in public, interacting with your baby, whilst out, has become more difficult and a little bit sad really. Sonny doesn't understand what my words mean just yet, but he does understand if I'm smiling at him. He will smile back at me every single time, and if he's crying, I will use my facial expressions to try and distract and comfort him.

When I've been out in public with him, all he can see are my eyes. I try and be as animated as possible with them but it's not the same. My face is different when it's covered by a face mask. He knows it's me but is clearly confused with how different I look. It's not familiar and he often just stares at me, puzzled, when I'm wearing my mask. All the research surrounding baby and child development show the importance of interacting with your baby, with them looking at you whilst they're in the pram and for you to just give them as much eye contact and interaction as possible.

Of course, Sonny could still hear me and see my eyes but it was just so unfamiliar to me and not what he was used to seeing at home. It was alien to me to be covered up and I would still smile my biggest smile to him, whilst he was in the pram and we were waiting at the school gates, completely forgetting my smile was hidden under a mask and he couldn't see what I was doing. I don't worry that it's affected our bonding, I know how much he loves and recognises me, but I feel so sad that if I need to comfort him, I can't in the way that he needs or that necessarily comes naturally to me. He knows no different of course, but when your baby is crying you want to be able to pull a comforting face and it's just sad that his first few months or years, when gathering these precious bonding moments, are with me behind a mask.

Not only have most organised baby classes been cancelled, but non organised activities have been too. I took my other sons swimming from such a young age and they loved nothing more than being dunked in a pool and splashing around until their fingers and toes pruned up. Sonny has never been swimming which is such a shame as he absolutely lives for bath time! He laughs and splashes and squeals and I just know he is my third little water baby and it's such a shame we can't take him for a swim.

When I was pregnant, I bought a cute, little swimming all-in-one and some swimming nappies. He has outgrown them all and it's just a shame they didn't get to be used even once. I can't wait to take Sonny swimming and although I'm sure he will absolutely love it, and join in with his brothers splashing around, I do worry that if we leave it too long, he'll get nervous. I always took my others swimming from newborn so it was never a scary experience for them and it was always considered normal.

Baby sensory was another beneficial session I used to enjoy taking my other two children to from when they were newborn. Although I know I can still take Sonny when he's an older baby, he's not been able to access it as a tiny baby. The days when they can just make out shapes and light is such a relaxing and therapeutic time to take them to baby sensory. Our children's centres have a sensory room that you can pre book for just you and baby, or to invite a few baby friends for a sensory hour. That had to stop with Covid which was a real shame. It did inspire me to get creative, though. I bought a foil blanket and a night light, poked some holes in to a cardboard box and made Sonny his own little sensory den. It was something a lot of the mums on our due date Facebook group did and it was lovely to see photographs of everybody's set ups and share ideas with others.

Not that Sonny cared or even noticed, but I missed being able to take him on little adventures or weekend getaways. Not that the idea of putting him in a car seat filled me with anything but dread, but had Covid not happened, and he used his car seat more often, he may not be so adverse to it. We'll never know; but I did miss taking him anywhere new. Whether it be the grandparents for the weekend or a day trip to the coast. Packing him a bag, choosing his favourite outfits and just altogether getting in some more firsts. Even things like taking him to the local aquarium which would be a sensory experience in itself had to be put on hold. I look forward to being able to do that soon.

I remember looking at Sonny once and seeing a rash on his tummy. I immediately put it down to one of those newborn rashes or because he'd recently had a bath and perhaps his skin had become a little irritated, but I remember thinking how scary and uncertain other parents might have felt in a similar situation in these times. There was a campaign at the time reminding people they could still use and access emergency services, and not to be put off because of Covid; but I do know of people and am sure there were many others that once upon a time would have got every little bump and rash checked but because of the times we were in, they were less eager to get it checked.

Appointments in general were harder to make and I do think it put people off coming forward if they were worried. A rash like the one I saw on Sonny, if it hadn't got worse or he'd not become unwell with it, I'd have saved it until the next health visitor clinic and popped by and mentioned it to them. I'd have probably taken a photo of it so I could show it to them the next time I was able to see them. Because services were a little harder to access now, I just left it. My gut and experience told me it was nothing to worry about, but I am sure there were thousands of parents in a similar situation where they had a niggling worry that they wouldn't mind running past a health care professional but that wasn't so bad that they had to make an appointment.

I, and so many others I know, were terrified of stepping foot in to a doctor's surgery or hospital at that point, particularly with a newborn, because of all the sick people and germs. It really was a final resort type situation and I can only empathise with people for the anxiety and worry it caused. Parents or not. Wanting to get an ailment checked but being too scared to isn't an ideal situation at all.

My heart always broke for Rory in particular when he would ask for the simplest of requests but that I couldn't carry out, because of a Covid restriction. He's only three, so can't comprehend the current situation. Archie understood that there were a lot of things we couldn't do just now, Rory is too young. This meant for the most part, Rory was blissfully ignorant and was just so happy to spend time with us all (especially his big brother) but when we were talking about what we should get up to the next day and he suggested we go to GaGa's house, it was just heart wrenching.

It's easier (not easy, but easier) to explain why I had to say no to soft play every time he asked about it but finding an explanation to why we couldn't see his grandparents was just awful. I know I'm not alone in this (and one of my beautiful friends is really struggling with this) but I do worry that when restrictions are lifted that the children will struggle socially. That they'll become withdrawn, confused (we are constantly telling them to put hand sanitiser on and not to get too close to people — it'll be a big change when they don't need to do that any more) and generally struggle to connect with people when life gets back to normal. I know in my heart they'll be fine. Children are resilient, I know this. But as a mother, none of this makes any of it any easier. What I would give to take him to the farm or the beach for the day, with a picnic and with grandparents and family and friends. One day. I just hope it's sooner rather than later so they can get back to enjoying the rest of their childhood.

They say it takes a village to raise a child. When living through a pandemic and instructed to stay at home, that village is taken away. Whether it be parents, friends, neighbours, colleagues, school run mums, health care staff or anyone else who makes up part of your day, without any of that your village reduces significantly. There would be nobody to hold the baby whilst I had a shower, nobody to cry to when I was exhausted and had a stressful day, just nobody to be there. At times it was an incredibly lonely existence. I had my three, beautiful children and my eldest can chat for England but it's just not the same as having a friend or family member over to be there for support and companionship. Some days were hard. Really hard.

Chapter Forty-One
Positivity and Perspective

THERE were lots of positives, too.

It's cathartic to write about all the ways the pandemic affected pregnancy and the newborn days. It was a unique time and all of those who went through this are part of a unique club, and will know this isn't moaning about it rather than a healthy release of our frustrations. Amongst all of the negatives and frustrations however, there were lots of positives; lots, actually. Here goes:

- Less diesel usage/costs
- No soggy school runs
- Exploring our local area
- Finding enjoyment and excitement in having no plans
- No colds/sickness bugs that came with having a child at primary school
- Seeing and hearing my son's lessons being taught
- Quieter roads
- Getting to know my children really well
- NO BRA!
- Learning how to enjoy a quieter pace of life
- Being able to spend uninterrupted time bonding with the baby
- Not having to share baby snuggles. We got him all to ourselves
- Getting enjoyment from our daily walks and not

walking to get to a particular destination
- It being sociably acceptable to answer the door in pyjamas
- Teaching my sons the value of playing with what we have at home
- Not having to deal with the stresses that come with after school activities

Most of these points come with a counter negative point (the last one for example- my son misses these classes so much so I would of course trade the negative for a positive in a heartbeat) but it's nice to focus on the positives as well as recognising the frustrations.

Lockdown 2.0 and 3.0 both came when I had a newborn. Ignoring all of the negatives that came with this, we were actually given the most beautiful distraction from the outside world. We got to stay in our newborn bubble and just be wholly consumed by a new little human.

Where so many others were struggling with how their social lives had changed, we were embracing how safe and cosy our nest was and really did have the best distraction.

On a whole, it has made us all appreciate family time so much more and has definitely reminded us all what's important. We've always valued spending time with our wider family, as touched upon before we don't have them for childcare or close enough to just pop in on, but this prolonged period of not being able to have family close to us has been so very hard, I'm not sure we'll let them go when we finally can see them again.

We had our health and so did our friends and family and of course, that is all I could ever hope for. At the time of writing, none of us (myself, husband or children) had had to have a Covid test, which was a miracle in itself. People were being tested left, right and centre as you had to be if you had any symptoms. With my husband working in a hospital, we were shocked that so far we had avoided any illness or need to be tested. It was amazing how good our health was; I think that was mainly due to no school germs! Our wider family had managed to stay well too and of course this was all we wanted. We had friends who had contracted Covid and although unwell at the time of having it, they made a full recovery. An old friend's father was sadly not as fortunate, and he lost his life to Covid.

Reports worldwide and the statistics of rising deaths were staggering. It was a terrifying time to be raising a family in and none of this was lost on me. I am fully aware that the hardships faced when pregnant and having a newborn were absolutely nothing in comparison to contracting Covid. I know this. As always, this is just my account of this specific time of my life and how Covid affected this.

There were so many times throughout my pregnancy and newborn days that were frustrating, disappointing and difficult. But overall, it wasn't really a hardship. Not compared to what thousands of others were going through. I had mainly a straightforward pregnancy, none of us became unwell or contracted Covid, my husband was able to continue working and we managed to home-school (mainly) successfully. We kept up our spirits, we explored new places and although we were kept from our friends and family like so much of the country, I really couldn't complain. There were so many positives to be taken from the negatives, and although acknowledging the negatives was important and valid, I would try and focus and concentrate on the positives and be thankful for what we had.

Chapter Forty-Two
We Made It

THESE days were hard. For everyone, of course. But for the purpose of this book, it was hard for parents of newborns. It was unprecedented, unexpected and we weren't prepared for how to handle it. Pregnancy was lonely, but I think (I know I certainly did) we hoped that by the time baby was here, things would have settled down and life would be getting back to normal.

There have been an inordinate number of highs and lows throughout 2020 and beyond. The pandemic took so much away but it also gave us so much. We made memories to last a lifetime; learnt how to slow down and to make the best out of what we have. Material possessions have never been high on my list of priorities but even less so now. We were truly able to find the beauty and appreciation in the small things and really embrace family time.

I don't worry what the pandemic will do to Sonny emotionally; he's too young and all he's interested in is milk and his big brothers pulling goofy faces at him to make him belly laugh. He will always be a child of 2020, one that was born into a global pandemic and a group of babies that will go down in history.

Printed in Great Britain
by Amazon

21546929R00103